DAILY LIFE ORNAMENTED
THE MEDIEVAL PERSIAN CITY OF RAYY

TANYA TREPTOW

with the collaboration of

DONALD WHITCOMB

THE ORIENTAL INSTITUTE MUSEUM OF THE UNIVERSITY OF CHICAGO

Library of Congress Control Number: 2007926335
ISBN: 1-885923-51-1
ISBN: 978-1-885923-51-6

The Oriental Institute, Chicago

Oriental Institute Museum Publications No. 26

This volume has been published in conjunction with the exhibition Daily Life
Ornamented: The Medieval Persian City of Rayy, held at the Oriental Institute
Museum, University of Chicago, May 15–October 14, 2007.

Series Editors' Acknowledgments

Lindsay DeCarlo, Katie L. Johnson, Rana Mikati, and Marcy Montross
assisted in the production of this volume.

Published by The Oriental Institute of the University of Chicago
1155 East 58th Street
Chicago, Illinois 60637 USA
oi.uchicago.edu

Front Cover Illustration:
Collage of sherds from this book and the exhibitition Daily Life Ornamented.

Printed by M&G Graphics, Chicago, Illinois.

TABLE OF CONTENTS

FOREWORD

GEOFF EMBERLING
DIRECTOR, ORIENTAL INSTITUTE MUSEUM

Archaeologists work with broken fragments to build pictures of life in past societies. In many excavations, the most abundant fragments we work with are broken pieces of ceramic vessels and objects (we call them "sherds"), which we find by the thousands in a typical dig. And these sherds can tell us quite remarkable things about the past — when in history a site was occupied, what trade contacts it had, and what kinds of everyday activities people were doing there. We can also learn about technologies and how artisans learned and adopted technologies across large areas. The finest ceramics, of course, are true works of art that convey an aesthetic sense that we can appreciate hundreds or thousands of years later.

Daily Life Ornamented: The Medieval Persian City of Rayy shows how archaeologists work with sherds at the same time that it portrays aspects of life along the Silk Road during the ninth–fourteenth centuries. It must be said that although the exhibition is based largely on sherds, they are not only interesting as documents of medieval Islamic civilization, they are also among the most beautiful sherds in the collections of the Oriental Institute. The exhibition, and this catalogue, also represent an opportunity to re-examine the pioneering work of Erich Schmidt, who excavated the ancient site of Rayy during the mid-1930s.

This exhibition began with a fortunate conjuncture of ideas and opportunities. The first was the new interest in Islamic art inspired by the exhibition of the David Collection at the Smart Museum of Art of the University of Chicago and the exhibition of the Harvey B. Plotnick collection of Islamic ceramics at the Art Institute of Chicago. These exhibitions are beautiful presentations of Islamic art and provide an interesting counterpart to the archaeological approach of the Oriental Institute. Both the David Collection and the Art Institute of Chicago have contributed photos and paintings to this exhibition, for which we are most grateful.

By coincidence, Tanya Treptow had recently finished a Master's thesis at the University of Chicago on the presentation of Islamic archaeology in American museums. Further, she had studied the Rayy collections in the storerooms of the Oriental Institute and held a research position at the Art Institute of Chicago. Her work in bringing the excavations and the city of Rayy back to life are excellent examples of the archaeologist's craft.

It is a pleasure to thank Tanya Treptow and Don Whitcomb for curating the exhibition with such energy and creativity. Abbas Alizadeh assisted in describing the site of Rayy today. Within the Oriental Institute Museum, it is a pleasure to thank Emily Teeter (Exhibit Coordinator); Erik Lindahl, Andrew Furse, and Elizabeth Beggs (Preparators); Laura D'Alessandro, Alison Whyte, and Monica Hudak (Conservators); Helen McDonald (Registrar); Tom James (Curatorial Assistant); John Larson and Margaret Schröeder (Archivists); and Marcy Montross (Photographer). In the Oriental Institute Publications Office, Leslie Schramer deserves much of the credit for producing this beautiful book on such tight deadlines, Tom Urban contributed his calm wisdom and keen editorial skills, and Lindsay DeCarlo and Katie L. Johnson provided valuable assistance. Dianne Hanau-Strain of Hanau-Strain Associates was integrally involved in the exhibition design as well as graphics.

The exhibition and publication were partially funded by a grant from LaSalle Banks, to whom we are grateful for long-standing interest and support.

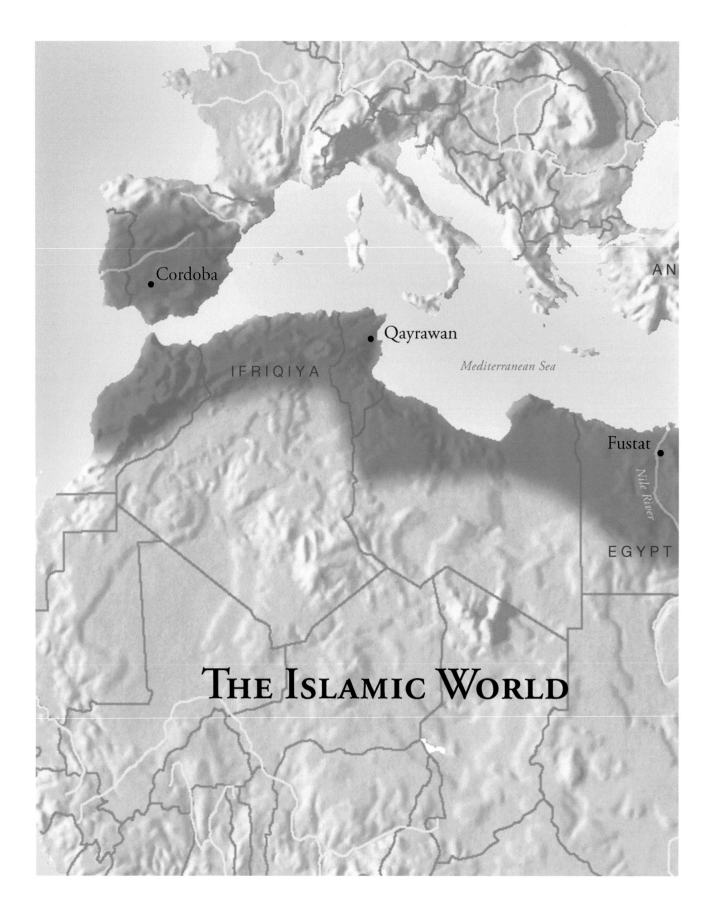

Map of the Islamic World

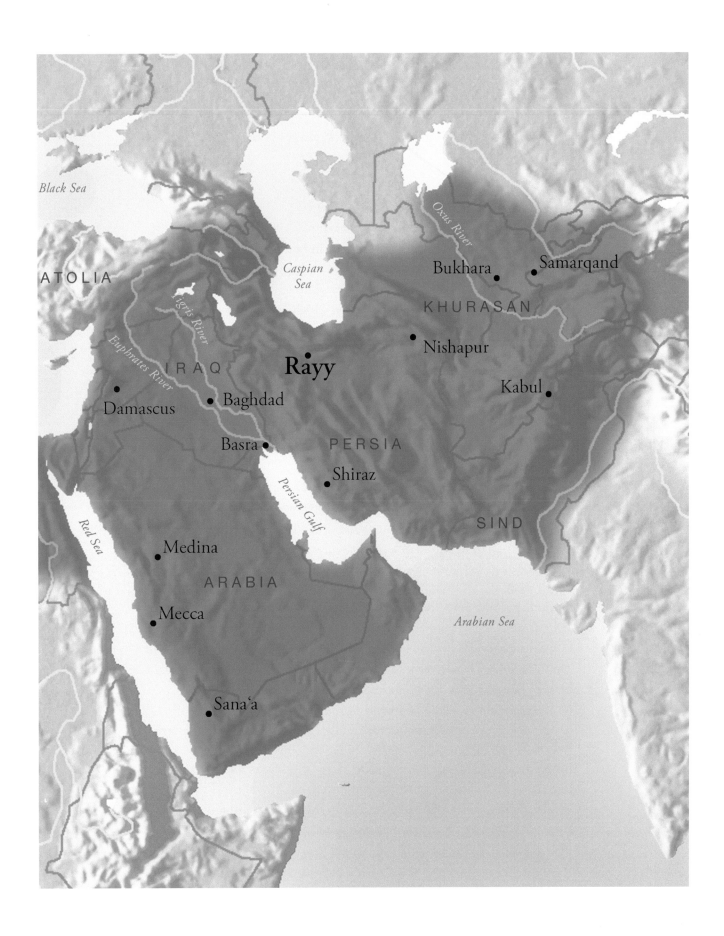

Black Sea

Caspian Sea

Oxus River

ATOLIA

Bukhara • • Samarqand

KHURASAN

Tigris River

Nishapur

Euphrates River

Rayy

IRAQ

Kabul •

Damascus • • Baghdad

Basra • PERSIA

Shiraz •

Persian Gulf

SIND

Red Sea

Medina •

ARABIA

Mecca •

Arabian Sea

Sana'a •

HISTORICAL TIME LINE OF RAYY

Bold type indicates significant events in the history of Rayy

B.C.

330   Alexander the Great camps at Rayy, then called "Rhages." His successors rebuild the town, calling it "Europos"

A.D.

ca. 430–490   Rayy is a bishopric of the Eastern Syrian Church

570–632   Life of Muhammad and the emergence of Islam

639–645   **Rayy is taken during the Islamic conquests, heralding the start of the Islamic period**

661–750   Expansion of the Islamic empire under the Umayyad dynasty, ruling from Damascus

750   Abbasid dynasty takes control from the Umayyads and moves the capital to Baghdad

774–775   **Al-Mahdi's Friday Mosque is built at Rayy, which is now called "al-Muhammadiya"**

786   Harun al-Rashid, born in Rayy, becomes Caliph of the Abbasid empire

863   Severe earthquake at Rayy; houses collapse and many people lose their lives

864 or later   Shah 'Abd al-Azim, a Shi'ite ascetic, dies at Rayy; his tomb becomes a venerated site for pilgrimage

916–917   Beginning of a confused period in the history of Rayy, during which the Samanids, the Abbasid caliphs, the Sadjites, and the local governors of Rayy compete for authority

947–948   **Rayy taken by the Buyid Rukn ud-Daulah; the Buyids rule as proxies for the Abbasids**

959   Earthquake at Rayy; much of the city is destroyed

985   The geographer al-Muqaddasi publishes an account of his travels including his visit to Rayy

ca. 1000   The poet Firdausi writes his famous epic of Iranian history, the *Shahnama*

ca. 1010   Ibn Sina (Avicenna), considered the father of modern medicine, takes residence at Rayy

1029   Rayy is captured by Mahmud of Ghazna, ending Buyid rule of the city

1038–39   Sack of Rayy by the Ghuzz Turks

1042–43   **Toghril, leader of the Seljuq Turks, finds the city of Rayy in ruins and orders it to be rebuilt; beginning of Seljuq rule at Rayy**

1071   Seljuq Turks begin to invade Anatolia and defeat the Byzantine army at Manzikert

1099   Europeans invade the Middle East and the First Crusade captures Jerusalem

1186–87   Civil strife at Rayy between the Sunnis and Shi'is; many killed and the city is left in ruins

ca. 1200   The poet Nizami writes his most famous work, the *Khamsa*

1220–21   The scholar Yaqut visits the city, which is mostly in ruins

1220–21   The Mongol army enters Rayy in pursuit of a rival leader; according to historical reports, the Mongols rob and plunder the city but do not remain long

1241   **Mongol armies again visit Rayy and the city is plundered and destroyed**

1271   Marco Polo sets sail from Venice, bound for China

1291   Crusaders forced to leave the Middle East by the Mamluk armies of Egypt

1301–02   A Mongol coin is struck at Rayy, indicating some revival of the city

1347   Bubonic plague in Europe

1404   A Spanish diplomat passes through Rayy and remarks that it is no longer inhabited

1453   Constantinople falls to the Ottoman Turks

1501   Beginning of the Safavid empire in Iran

1934–36   Rayy excavated by Erich Schmidt

RAYY: FROM WALLIS TO WATSON

There can be few archaeological sites of key Islamic interest that have undergone the trajectory that Rayy has suffered over the last century and a quarter. Suffered is the appropriate word – Rayy is a victim and through no fault of its own has seen its fortune dramatically decline. Once a place of towering authority and importance, the head of the family no less, it is now merely a place of probable but uncertain worth, a distant miserly aunt of unknown wealth. At least that is how it seems to us outsiders, and for more than a century most of us have been outsiders. This exhibition is a rare opportunity to peep into one of the few accessible vaults of Rayy's treasures.

Rayy, under its alternate name "Rhages," came to prominence as a historical site in the late nineteenth century when Islamic pottery had finally caught the enthusiastic attention of Western collectors both private and institutional. It was a natural site to claim attention, with its long history back to the third millennium B.C., maintaining its importance through the Parthian, Sasanian, and Islamic periods. For the pious in the West, it had the added attraction of being mentioned in the Apocrypha: Tobit sent his son Tobias from Nineveh to recover the silver deposited there (Tobit 1:14) and the book of Judith (1:15) puts near Rayy the plain where Nebuchadnezzar defeated the king of Media, Arphaxad.

More recently, Rayy has an importance in two ways: its ruins provided the richest source of early and medieval material for the art market, and among that material were two modest sherds of supreme documentary importance – ceramic wasters from kiln production, including one of lusterware. These were acquired by the British collector F. Godman and were illustrated in a lavish publication by Henry Wallis before being given to the British Museum in 1891.[1] The importance of the sherds was two-fold. As the only "wasters" known, they gave secure "archaeological" information about the provenance of Persian lusterware, one of the most sought-after wares of its day, and it was used as a key argument in the ferocious debate about who invented luster technique – Egypt or Iran.

So Rayy for a few glorious decades reigned supreme as the "attribution of choice" for dealers, collectors, and curators as they competed both in the art market and in academic publication. The contribution made by Rayy can be gauged from A. U. Pope's description: the site "... occupies at least ten square miles, and ... scarcely a square yard of this has been left untouched by previous commercial diggers. In 1930 after fifty years of excavation there were nearly a thousand diggers still working on it, often going to very deep levels."[2] So, although other sites were exhausted by the 1930s, Rayy still reigned supreme as the source of the best luster- and enameled *minai* wares. Most material, however, still arrived on the market with no secure attribution, just "said to be found at" on the say-so of the dealers who might be at several removes from the diggers themselves.

This state of affairs had been under attack for some time. The great German archaeologist F. Sarre complained vociferously as early as 1913 that the French who had a monopoly of excavations in Iran had abandoned Rayy to "the destruction and ruthless exploitation of local dealers" who were simply "grave-robbers representing Islamic archaeology."[3]

Others too had voiced concern over the lack of "scientific archaeology," for which reason the excavations by Erich Schmidt in the 1930s were particularly welcomed. Excavation might set Rayy's contribution on a firmer footing – for in the 1930s Rayy began to be considered less important. Pope had begun to speculate that other sites were as important – Saveh, Sultanabad, Zenjan among others, and especially Kashan. Particularly hard was the re-attribution from Rayy to Kashan of one of the finest styles of luster painting, first suggested by Pope, then authoritatively demonstrated by Richard Ettinghausen in 1936.[4] Rayy, however, continued to hold its position as a maker of certain styles of luster, and of *minai* and other wares.[5] In the 1970s, as a doctoral student, I showed that there was no evidence for lusterware production at the site; Wallis' famed waster was not a waster after all but just a "second," carrying no proof of local manufacture.[6] By comparison with more certain production in Kashan, evidence for *minai* and underglaze-painted wares at Rayy was also re-evaluated. In the end nothing certain remained there – just the hunch that so important a city must have had some local potters.

So now the current situation: a site, sadly reduced from its former glory, suffering from lack of secure information as to what was found there, with not a single ware securely attributed to its name, and the whole of the medieval luxury industry apparently handed to its former rival Kashan. We still suffer from a lack of scientific archaeology, as Schmidt's excavations were never published. But his finds — sherds and pots known to have been dug up in Rayy — exist as archive collections in Iran, Boston, Philadelphia, and Chicago. These have not been published either and have only been seen by a few researchers or students working on set term papers. Until now.

Let us hope this exhibition is the start of a revival of Rayy's fortunes: the beginning of an ongoing study and publication of the material found there, that we may finally know for certain what was used, and perhaps made, in this all-important of Persian medieval cities. The attribution of things to Rayy may again become fashionable, but this time with well-based confidence.

Dr. Oliver Watson
Ashmolean Museum, University of Oxford
March 2007

INTRODUCTION TO THE EXHIBITION

Archaeology is not limited to excavations and the discovery of artifacts. Most archaeological work is actually undertaken after crews return from a dig site during the process of analyzing finds and interpreting objects from the past. In this regard, some of the most exciting discoveries come out of the storerooms and basements of museums, where many archaeological collections reside for the long term.

The Oriental Institute of the University of Chicago facilitates this type of discovery on a daily basis. It is a treasure house for archaeological collections from all periods of the ancient Near East, and it is a forum for scholars and researchers who help catalogue and analyze its vast holdings. The Oriental Institute's collection of ceramics from the Persian city of Rayy still awaits a full discovery. Most of these ceramics are sherds which came to the Institute after excavations at Rayy in the 1930s, part of a larger collection of artifacts divided among several museums. Sadly, no detailed report of the excavations was published and this once-famous city has made little contribution to the growing discipline of Islamic archaeology. For these many years, Rayy's ceramics have been stored safely but quietly in dozens of boxes on basement shelves.

More fortunate, however, is that with good documentation and adequate care, the findings from archaeological sites are very durable and can be adapted to new research questions even decades after an original excavation. The ceramics from Rayy fit this example; although they have been more or less inaccessible up to the present, the results of the excavations are still largely recoverable. Daily Life Ornamented makes a purposeful attempt to highlight the future research potential of this collection, but it is not a definitive report of results from the excavations since the artifacts have not yet been fully analyzed. Instead, this exhibition presents Rayy's ceramics in a more general context, as a key to a better understanding of Islamic culture and as a taste of the beauty of everyday cosmopolitan life in a medieval Islamic city.

Rayy is well suited to begin a discussion of Islamic culture because of its unique location — still relevant in the modern world. The vast extent of the medieval walled city was to be the predecessor of modern Tehran, the current capital of Iran. The few surviving ruins of Rayy can still be seen today in the southern suburbs of Tehran, among growing plots of factories and other industrial buildings. In earlier times, this location held an important strategic position at the crossing of ancient Silk Roads, balanced between the Alburz mountain range of northern Iran and the high central Iranian plateau. It was settled over five thousand years ago,[7] grew into a thriving town, and eventually became the prosperous city which was often mentioned by historians of the Islamic era.

Erich Schmidt, the director of the excavations in the 1930s, was well aware of Rayy's medieval history, both as a political capital in the early Islamic period and as a center of scholarship from the ninth to the thirteenth centuries. Here the streets were walked by Harun al-Rashid, who went on to become the most famous caliph of the wide-reaching Abbasid empire, and libraries used by Ibn Sina before his philosophy attracted Western attention. Further, the city could boast of an observatory for astronomers and a hospital that advanced medical studies. As the geographer al-Muqaddasi noted in the tenth century, "the people have beauty, intelligence, honor, refinement. Here are councils and schools, natural talents, handicrafts...."[8]

Among the most renowned of Rayy's handicrafts were its glazed ceramics. During three seasons of excavations, from 1934 to 1936, Schmidt uncovered thousands of ceramic sherds that had been deposited in trash pits throughout Rayy's neighborhoods. In addition to wealthy patrons who promoted ceramic arts, ordinary families invested in beautiful ceramics for their private, daily lives at Rayy, and therefore all areas of the site yielded a wealth of ceramic material. These ceramics range in design from modest cooking wares to the finest luxury wares, but all reflect a fascination for decoration and have long attracted the attention of historians of Islamic art. Even everyday storage vessels have patterns of incised decoration or added bits of glaze as a colorful mosaic. Rayy's ceramics are a part of local traditions of northern Iran, but many of their designs and decorations also link Rayy to a shared Islamic culture that spanned the Middle East.

Daily Life Ornamented provides an opportunity to present both the striking aesthetics of Rayy's ceramics and — through their archaeological context — a picture of Islamic culture as the source of their amazing variety of ornamentation. It is hoped that these objects will enrich everyone's understanding and appreciation of Islamic society, especially at a time when so many negative associations are fostered on the cultures of the Middle East.

In Daily Life Ornamented the theme of ornamentation acts as a guide through archaeology toward an understanding of Rayy as both the source and the consumer of beauty in everyday life. Many of the ceramics in this exhibition, which come from Schmidt's excavations at Rayy, have never before been publicly displayed. The original watercolor paintings and photographs used to document the Rayy excavations complement the ceramic material. Several Persian miniature paintings from the Art Institute of Chicago also help visitors to visualize the important uses of medieval ceramics from the perspective of contemporary eyes. We hope that visitors enjoy the experience, and that Rayy's ceramics illuminate the cultural heritage of the Middle East while demonstrating how even the humble potsherd has a role to play in our exploration of earlier peoples and civilizations.

ERICH SCHMIDT'S EXCAVATIONS AT RAYY

The ruins of Rayy were famous long before any scientific excavations were begun. For the past six to seven hundred years, the ruins have been a literal gold mine for treasure hunters who sought precious metals hidden or left by the people of Rayy in times of crisis. However, digging was deeply intensified in the nineteenth century due to a growing European interest in Islamic lands and willingness to pay for objects of Islamic art. The focus was no longer on gold, but instead on golden-glazed and brightly colored ceramic wares that were highly valued in the expanding art market. Rayy quickly became pockmarked with trenches made by the activities of pot-hunters, a trend that lasted well into the twentieth century.

Increasing Western access to the Middle East in the nineteenth century also resulted in a more scholarly interest in the ruins of Rayy. Europeans first "discovered" Rayy through the efforts of diplomats who were also travelers and explorers. The earliest accounts come from British travelers such as J. Morier, Robert Ker Porter, and Sir W. Ousely, each of whom made independent visits to Rayy in the 1810s and 1820s.[9] Although their descriptions are often filled with an unconcealed romance for the faded ruins of an ancient land, these men were also well informed about the growing body of scholarship on Rayy's historical past. Their writings are much more than travelers' accounts and they preserve descriptions of monuments that are now destroyed and some of the first maps of the ruins.

THE ROMANTIC APPEAL OF AN ANCIENT CITY

Sir Robert Ker Porter gives us a first-hand perspective of the mystique that Rayy held for an early European visitor. By this time scholars were well versed in Rayy's history, and this account refers to both early Persian and biblical sources. The reference to an angel and a prophet likely describes a story from the Book of Tobias in the Christian Apocrypha, where the angel Raphael guides the son of Tobias to Rayy (5:1–22).

> The names of Rhages, Europa, Arsacia, and Rhey, have all, at different periods, designated this ancient metropolis; each name giving just grounds for anticipating the richest succession of antiquities, if curiosity might be permitted to explore the huge mounds which cover its buried remains. The Persians ascribe its origin to Houshong, the grandson of Kaiomurs; therefore, only third in descent from the first monarch of that dynasty, who, by every calculation, must have been several centuries before the age of Cyrus...
>
> In calculating the antiquity of its foundation, even the exaggerating traditions of the Persian poets may not have far exceeded the truth. Rhey has, at different times, been the residence of the sovereigns of the empire; or, as the capital of a province, of its own Prince-governors. It has been distinguished with palaces; it has been sanctified by fire-temples, or mosques; it has been elevated by one conqueror, to the honours of a capital; it has been sacked by the next, as only worthy of his vengeance. Hence, the city which an angel and a prophet blessed with their presence, is now become a scene of such desolation, that the footsteps of man are hardly discernible, except where they have left traces of war and mark his grave...
>
> However, as I am not aware of even the few noble relics which yet remain, having been particularly described by any European traveler, I shall attempt a sketch of what I saw. The ruins lie about five miles south-east of Tehran, extending from the foot of the curving mountains, and running in that direction across the plain in an oblique line south-west. The surface of the ground, all over this tract, is marked by hollows, mounds, mouldering towers, tombs, and wells. The fabric of all, being chiefly of that burnt, and sun-dried material, which seems to bid defiance to the last oblivious touch of time....
>
> — Porter, *Travels in Georgia*, vol. 1, pp. 357-58

Even with these early accounts of Rayy, the physical structure of the half-buried city and exact origin of ceramic wares remained tantalizingly inaccessible to scholars. This frustration combined with a growing outrage over unscientific digging at the site and eventually culminated in firm plans for a systematic archaeological excavation. Rayy was first excavated from 1934 to 1936 as a cooperative project between the Museum of Fine Arts in Boston and the Mrs. William Boyce Thompson Foundation of the University of Pennsylvania. The excavations were directed by Erich Schmidt, a German-American archaeologist who is best known for his scientific excavations of the great ruins of Persepolis.

ERICH SCHMIDT'S EXCAVATION STRATEGY AT RAYY

Erich Schmidt chose Rayy as a center of excavation activities because one of his main scientific goals was to achieve a cultural cross section of the historical periods of Persia. This city was an obvious choice for Schmidt because of its "key geographical position at the crossing of ancient routes from north to south and east to west, and its importance from Median times to the final destruction by Tamerlane."[10] Of course, Schmidt was also intrigued by the "famous glazed ceramics" of Rayy. He hoped to clarify the dating and basic typology for these pottery types by analyzing archaeological data.

At the start of the excavations, the main boundary of the medieval city of Rayy — its impressive system of fortified walls — was still largely visible, as was the general layout of the city. Large sections of the city walls remained standing, along with several bastions and towers, which gave the plan of the city an irregular triangular shape. At the heart of the fortifications, at a corner of this triangle, a strong citadel occupied a promontory of rock jutting out from the mountains that bordered the eastern edge of the plain. From the citadel, the central walled metropolis of Rayy radiated over a mile toward the south and the west.

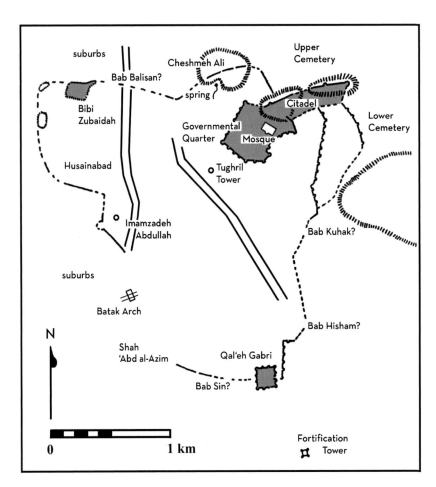

Site map of the Islamic city of Rayy

ERICH SCHMIDT

Erich Schmidt may very well have been the busiest Western archaeologist working in Iran during the 1930s. He directed the excavation of the mounds of Rayy from 1934 to 1936, under the auspices of the University Museum of the University of Pennsylvania and the Museum of Fine Arts, Boston. With the financial assistance and support of his wife, Mary-Helen Warden, and her parents, Schmidt established the Aerial Survey of Iran, which was intended to be a comprehensive survey of the archaeological sites in Iran — a combination of aerial photography and observations made on the ground.

In 1935, Schmidt replaced Ernst E. Herzfeld as field director of the Persepolis Expedition of the Oriental Institute of the University of Chicago, in which capacity he served through the end of 1939. In 1935 and 1938, Schmidt was also seconded to direct the Oriental Institute's Holmes Expeditions to Luristan. The records generated by the personnel of all four projects, now housed in the Oriental Institute Archives, exhibit an especially high standard of archaeological field recording for the 1930s and are noteworthy for the extensive use of photography, as well as for the production of numerous sketches and drawings of the objects found.

By the 1930s, most of Rayy's vast network of markets, streets, and neighborhoods were mostly buried by layers of soil brought to the plain by yearly floods.[11] Because of these deposits, much of the medieval city was difficult to recognize and the best placement for excavations became a tricky decision. However, a few areas of the ancient city stood out above the plain. The Cheshmeh Ali mound and the Citadel, both located on rocky outcrops at the northern end of the city, were two of these areas, and very promising for excavation. In addition, one particular quarter of the city remained distinct: the section nearest the Citadel was set apart by a large wall. All these areas — in addition to test pits throughout the lower areas of the larger city — were the early foci of Schmidt's excavations.

Even in areas that were recognized as important, acquiring permission to excavate was often difficult. Although the inner city of Rayy was mostly abandoned after the Mongol raids of Genghis Khan in the thirteenth century, settlement in the plain had never stopped. Slightly to the north, the village of Tehran had grown into a large city. Directly to the south of Rayy's medieval walls, another village had formed around the shrine of Shah 'Abd al-Azim, a Shi'ite ascetic who died at Rayy in the ninth century. By the 1930s, the village of Shah 'Abd al-Azim had encroached onto the archaeological remains; this meant that most of the archaeological site was under private ownership and much of it was being used for agriculture.

Negotiations between the excavators and land owners consumed much initial time and effort. Schmidt often resorted to explicit help from the Iranian government and was able to have some areas of Rayy registered as a national monument. In most cases, the excavators tried to refrain from digging in agriculturally valuable ground, which reduced, but did not always eliminate, the friction with property owners.[12] Obviously, these issues were at the front of Schmidt's thoughts in addition to his scientific goals, but he managed to balance between these poles surprisingly well and was able to cover a wide area of excavation over three seasons.

Schmidt employed several hundred workers for the excavations at Rayy, the majority of whom were native Iranians along with some outside specialists. Since the site was so large, the expedition sounded out many different areas in order to gain a general appreciation for the scope and time frame of the site. Schmidt's coordination of the excavation was an impressive feat. Workers were split into several crews assigned to excavate in the different areas and were shifted or rejoined wherever extra hands were most needed throughout the excavation seasons. At some points, over two hundred workers might be digging together in the same area of the site.

Although the excavated areas were many square meters in area and larger than excavations at most archaeological sites today, at the time they were smaller than other typical large-scale excavations in the Middle East. In part, Schmidt's excavations were limited because of the complexity and depth of Islamic strata at Rayy:

> As a rule, Rayy has no distinct architectural levels. The house remains of the Islamic era are almost hopelessly involved and mostly sterile. But the trash pits, hundreds of thousands of which must pierce the ancient city, supply the beautiful vessels of Abbasid and Saljuq times and the scientific data concerning the development of the city and its handicrafts. — Schmidt, "Rayy Spring Season 1936"

The results of the excavations at Rayy were expected to benefit multiple academic institutions, although primarily to enhance the collections of the sponsoring museums. Erich Schmidt also received assistance from the Iranian government, and in accordance with newly established antiquities laws, half of the material recovered from the excavations was retained by Iranian museums.[13] Despite its leanings toward the acquisition of art, the excavation of Rayy was conducted in a scientific way to document stratigraphy and archaeological relationships, which Schmidt recorded in detail in many large notebooks.

During the expedition, the different sectors of the Islamic city became a main focus for research, but it is important to remember they were not Schmidt's only focus. The excavation team also gave attention to the late Neolithic and Chalcolithic mound of Cheshmeh Ali at the edge of the city, as well as a nearby palace structure called Chal Tarkhan, a tomb construction to the east called Naqqareh Khaneh, and other prehistoric sites to the west. These various efforts each deserve individual publications and cannot be effectively addressed in this exhibition, where the focus is on Islamic remains inside the city walls. Since Schmidt's excavation reports are not easily accessible, a brief summary of the Islamic remains inside the city walls is provided here.

We broke ground at the Citadel on May 16 [1935] in an area of 400 square meters on the eastern flat part of the hill. The base of fortress was 15 meters below fading into the so-called Governmental Quarters, while outer city defense walls extend in the form of eccentric circles from other points of the fortress far into the plain... The fact that an occupational level of the middle of the eleventh century underlies remains of the fifteenth century indicates that during the time of the greatest splendor, namely, the Saljuq period, of Rayy that part of the citadel which we are testing was not occupied.

— Schmidt, "Rayy Excavations – Season 1935"

Previously we called this area the Saljuq Center. It is true, the most attractive Saljuq vessels were found at this spot; but, in addition, excellent examples of Early Islamic pottery also occur in this suburb of modern Shah 'Abd al-Azim... There are bowls of the famous Abbasid "Samarra" type, elegant bottles and jars, gold luster bowls of the Middle Islamic period and the most lovely of all Persian ceramics, the minai vessels in polychrome enamels.

— Schmidt, "Rayy Spring Season 1936"

When the aerial photographs, mapping the citadel and the so-called Governmental Quarter of Rayy, were examined and analyzed, an area in the quarter below the citadel appeared so interesting that we proceeded to test it. The stuccos here illustrated are the result of this test. The construction of the building, namely, ornamented rooms opening into a large court, together with the unusual sterility as to pits and there with remains of domestic objects, defined the building as a religious or governmental building. For the moment we believe that it was a religious school. In addition to the white stuccos decorating the front row of rooms, fragments of painted, even gilded, plaster occurred in the second tier.

— Schmidt, "Rayy Spring Season 1936"

A SHORT SUMMARY OF THREE SEASONS OF EXCAVATION 1934-36

During the first season of fieldwork in 1934, Schmidt opened a number of excavations and test pits in order to obtain a stratigraphical sequence for as many periods of settlement at Rayy as possible. These pits were continually expanded throughout the expedition because of the depth of settlement at Rayy. At first, excavations were restricted to the Cheshmeh Ali mound at the northern edge of the city because of ownership problems in other potential excavation areas. Nine excavation squares (totaling 900 square meters) were begun in the southern part of the mound. Here, excavators uncovered Islamic burials and mausoleums and a section of a Parthian palace.

Soon, Schmidt obtained more digging rights, and excavations began in several more areas: at Qal'eh Gabri along the south wall of the city, at a tomb tower near the city edge, and at an area of Seljuq (eleventh–thirteenth centuries) settlement near the ruined sanctuary of Bibi Zubaidah in the center of the city. These areas consisted of Islamic periods of occupation with a few pre-Islamic remains. After a brief period of excavation, half of the excavation crew was pulled from these areas to begin additional explorations directly below the Citadel mound in the small area walled off from the larger city. Schmidt called this area the "Governmental Quarter"[14] because of the larger buildings found there. The main goal of excavation in the Governmental Quarter was to uncover a structure identified as a large mosque.

The second season continued Schmidt's focus on obtaining an entire sequence of occupation as well as more detailed chronologies. Excavations continued into prehistoric levels on the Cheshmeh Ali mound. Excavators also opened a large area on the Citadel mound in order to get another long-term sequence of settlement. Schmidt hoped to encounter Islamic palatial structures of the Seljuq period by starting new excavations in the garden of Abul Fath Zadeh to the south of the Citadel and Governmental Quarter but still within the city walls.[15] Here, they excavated an area of over 600 square meters. Although they did not discover palatial structures, they discovered many well-defined buildings, probably house structures, with vaulted, semi-subterranean storerooms and refuse pits, as well as very large amounts of glazed pottery and other artifacts.

During the third season, "the clear original program ... had been upset in almost every feature, due to delays and interferences beyond our control."[16] However, Schmidt was still able to expand excavations into related sites beyond the city walls and also continue many previous areas of excavation. Excavations and restorations were conducted at the tomb construction of Naqqareh Khaneh to the east of the main city. Schmidt was also able to come to an agreement with the owners of the ruin of Chal Tarkhan palace and begin excavations. Within Rayy, work continued at both the Cheshmeh Ali mound and the Citadel, and a structure tentatively identified as a *madrasa* (a religious school) was located in the Governmental Quarter. Additional areas of Seljuq settlement in Husainabad were excavated in order to establish better chronologies of Islamic pottery and acquire more museum pieces.

Although excavations at Rayy were completed successfully, a full report of these efforts was never completed due to outside forces such as the Second World War and Erich Schmidt's unexpected death in 1964. The collection of artifacts is now divided among several museums, with the majority in Tehran and Pennsylvania. The Oriental Institute's collection of ceramics can only be considered a sample of the archaeological wealth from Rayy. However, Schmidt's detailed records of the excavations remain intact at the Oriental Institute, preserving the context of all recorded artifacts. They include preliminary reports, typologies, photographs, as well as a number of surprisingly sophisticated watercolor paintings of the most artistically crafted ceramics and glass vessels.

DISCOVERING ISLAMIC CULTURE: AN ARCHAEOLOGIST'S PERSPECTIVE

Most museum collections of Islamic ceramics have been gathered from dealers, private collections, and donations. These acquisitions provide an impressive overview of the artistic periods and regions of Islamic culture, but information on the background of individual pieces is often uncertain. Through a thriving and often anonymous 150-year art market, many objects have lost all records of where they were originally found. It is rare to view Islamic ceramics, such as those excavated at Rayy, that have direct connections to the people who might have originally used and valued them.

The ceramics on display in Daily Life Ornamented are an expression of a shared way of life that emerged at Rayy in the early medieval period when innovations in ceramic design and decoration began to meld into a common tradition throughout the Middle East. In fact, ceramics are just one example of this phenomenon, which is reflected in other media such as architecture, metalwork, glassmaking, and even the organization of cities. These traditions met the needs of a new community which spanned political and ethnic boundaries. Modern scholars often identify this common society of the Middle East as "Islamic culture."

While there is no one comprehensive definition of culture, scholars generally see it as a system of shared knowledge, values, and attitudes which create a common experience of life and a framework for behavior. For many people, the term "Islamic culture" has an obvious connotation of religious practice, and indeed the religion of Islam (established in the seventh century) inspired many aspects of life at Rayy in the medieval period. However, Islamic culture is usually defined as a larger system which shaped all aspects of life, both secular and religious, in regions ruled by Muslim governments or regions with a significant Muslim population. It is a unique concept that skirts modern attempts of compartmentalization. It is neither a geographical reference (like "European" history) nor a strictly religious one (like "Buddhist" art) but can be more comfortably categorized as a social community. This meaning is closely reflected in medieval Rayy, as well as much of the Middle East during the same time period and beyond — especially since Islamic culture is still very much a presence in today's modern world. But what did Islamic culture mean in practice? And how did it impact the lives of people living at Rayy?

AN ARCHAEOLOGIST'S EYE: SEEING THE WHOLE IN A PART

Scholars often study cultures of the past by examining historical documents to see what people wrote about their lives. The presence of culture is often very elusive in these documents, however, because they only describe life from one person's perspective, the chronicler's. People — both past and present — are often so enmeshed in the patterns of their culture that they take it for granted as "the way life is." Many historical writers also considered aspects of their culture to be so well known to their contemporary readers that they felt no need to give explanations, leaving modern scholars guessing the real meaning of metaphors, allusions, and other references. Essentially, what people wrote does not always reveal how they lived.

Another source for culture is archaeological material remains, such as the ceramics which had a familiar place in the lives of many of Rayy's residents. Like historical scholarship, archaeology helps scholars reach toward an understanding of culture by indirect means. Through archaeology, patterns of artifacts are first interpreted as reflections of behavior. Individual behaviors are then connected to the shared experiences of larger groups and the boundaries of culture are visualized.

Artifacts are the key to this process, which is why they are often called "material culture." An archaeologist starts out with only bits and pieces of material culture, fragmentary in almost every way. For example, most of the objects from the Rayy excavations had been lying in the earth for hundreds, sometimes thousands of years. These objects often look very different from when they were in use. Many are broken or have deteriorated after years underground, and understanding them as they originally were created — as new, whole objects — is an act of imagination.[17] Anyone who wants to appreciate archaeological artifacts needs to train their eyes to recognize them.

Left: Fritware jar sherd, luster painted over opaque white glaze outside and blue glaze inside (OIM A115073); watercolor reconstruction of whole vessel, artist unknown (Oriental Institute, RH 5612)
Middle: Base of fritware vessel decorated with *minai* technique over opaque white glaze (OIM A115208); watercolor reconstruction of complete piece, artist unknown (Oriental Institute, RH 6064)
Right: Central base of fritware lamp with turquoise glaze (OIM A115080); watercolor reconstruction of complete lamp, artist unknown (Oriental Institute, RE 3114)

The three artifacts above (OIM A115073, A115208, A115080) are good examples of how archaeologists gradually develop the ability to see a fragment and visualize a whole. Archaeologists use the term "sherd" to describe broken ceramic pieces. While each of these sherds has some type of design and a particular shape, most people would have difficulty making any sort of visual sense out of them. However, once you compare them with similar whole objects, the small fragments immediately become recognizable. Splotches of brown become curving arabesques along the smooth walls of a vase. A jumble of intertwined gray lines becomes the central medallion of a large bowl. A strange spout becomes the pedestal for an elegant lamp. The importance of training the eyes in this way is that these comparisons remain in long-term memory. If the whole objects are removed, most people can still mentally picture what part of an object each sherd is from and even recognize other fragments that are similar. Although professional archaeologists often monopolize this process in the early stages of archaeological research, anyone can learn this skill and begin their own discovery of artifacts from sherds.

Another useful technique for recognizing an artifact fragment as part of a whole is looking at the range of forms of a particular type of object. A "typology" is a systematic classification of things that have traits in common. The objects pictured at left, for example, are whole or fragmentary lanterns found at Islamic Rayy. These lanterns might have different types of handles and bases, but they all have a basin for holding oil and a small spout to support a lighted wick. Typologies are critical in archaeological research because they help organize a mass of detail, for example, the thousands of artifacts that might be found during

Clockwise from top left: Watercolor of lamp with turquoise glaze, artist unknown (Oriental Institute, RH 5039); earthenware lamp with turquoise glaze (OIM A115005); body and handle (pieces do not join) of earthen lamp with turquoise glaze (OIM A115074 [body], A115082 [handle]); watercolor of lamp with green glaze, artist unknown (Oriental Institute, RE 2763)

MAKING COMPARISONS ARCHAEOLOGY AND ART

Islamic artists used a decorative repertoire of conventional themes, therefore even if only a small part of a decoration survives, it is often possible to recover its meaning. This round tapestry from the David Collection, Copenhagen, depicts a Mongol ruler seated on a low throne, a parasol above his head. He is attended by Mongol soldiers and a seated officer, who appears to converse with a Muslim courtier. The style of the courtly scene on this tapestry is thought to come from Central Asia and to date to the fourteenth century.

There is a small sherd of *minai*-painted ware in the Rayy collection that makes an instructive comparison. The sherd is a very small part of a scene, rather difficult to understand by itself, which fits comfortably into the larger scene on the tapestry. When seen in conjunction with the sherd is revealed as a part of a standard court scene, even to the bird strutting in the foreground. The parallel is quite close, even to the structure of the throne and colored pattern on the ruler's vestment.

These identical scenes are possible only if one flips the tapestry over, revealing it to be a reverse of the sherd. This may imply that the common origin may have been a copy-book, carried by itinerant artists. More importantly, the sherd from Rayy was a bowl used (and broken) in that city in the late twelfth or early thirteenth century. One may thus suggest the archaeological context establishes the scene as one common to a Persian medieval repertoire and adapted to textile for another context.

Top left: Base of fritware vessel decorated with *minai* technique over opaque white glaze. OIM A115007
Right: Tapestry roundel. First half of fourteenth century, Central Asia. Silk and gold thread woven on cotton core. Diameter 69 cm. The David Collection, Copenhagen. 30/1995
Bottom left: Fritware sherd superimposed on reversed tapestry

excavations at a site. An archaeologist who has studied artifacts typologies can often pick up a small fragment of pottery from the ground and determine what object it came from and approximately when it was used. Typologies also make very useful points of comparison between archaeological sites. Since no one can personally view all the artifacts from all the Islamic sites ever excavated, published drawings of artifacts organized by typology make the findings of archaeology accessible to everyone.

PUTTING IT ALL TOGETHER

The excavating team at Rayy became so familiar with the bits and pieces of Islamic pottery at the site that they were able to do more than imagine the original state of the whole objects. They were often able to reconstruct the original pot or bowl from a number of small sherds. Erich Schmidt, the director of the excavations, explains:

> Out of hundreds of thousands of fragments, carefully separated as to find locations, our expert restorers assemble, in the course of the season, the delightful vessels of the Islamic era. The character of the findspots, namely the trashpits, explains that most vessels had been broken and discarded during the occupation of the site. Thus, it rarely happens that complete specimens are found. On the other hand, in many cases the restorers succeed to assemble all fragments of vessels which, at one time, had been scattered in various pits and rooms. — Schmidt, "Rayy Spring Season 1936"

While a common perception of an archaeologist's work is the task of putting together an artifact piece by piece, reconstructing ceramics is only the first step of archaeological investigations. The real work begins with interpreting how ceramics were made and used and why they were made in particular ways, so that they best reflect the behavior of people and the framework of cultures. Fortunately, archaeology provides a number of tools to help build up this picture. One of the greatest benefits of examining an archaeological collection of ceramics is knowing its "context" (also called stratigraphy), the location where each object was excavated and its relation to the objects and buildings around it. All archaeological analyses and interpretations build upon this basic knowledge, which is why it is so important to preserve excavation records.

Archaeological context is fundamental for what it can reveal about Rayy itself. Rayy's ceramics reflect the actions of its people in many ways, but they illuminate most fully four main aspects of Islamic culture, which are explored in the different sections of this exhibition:

- Islamic culture was most vibrant in moments of everyday life at Rayy, where ceramics played a major role.
- Even in these intimate settings, Islamic society was a culture of connections which linked Rayy's neighborhoods to a wider world.
- The Islamic world was profoundly inspired by religion but was not limited to religious expressions.
- Islamic culture encouraged industry and innovation, for which Rayy was both a consumer and a source for new creativity.

Reconstruction of pottery during excavations at Rayy

CATALOGUE OF THE EXHIBITION

EVERYDAY BEAUTY

One of the most enchanting characteristics of Islamic material culture comes from the way that beauty and utility are closely intertwined in daily life. In European traditions, decorated but functional objects are often separated conceptually from more prestigious, forms of art such as sculpture and fine painting. However, the Islamic world makes much less of this distinction, with the effect that many of the finest craftsmen dedicated their efforts to the beautification of ceramics and other objects used in the activities of everyday life.[18]

This section of the exhibition takes an in-depth look at the role of decorated ceramics in one section of the city of Rayy, southwest of the Citadel mound. In the early twentieth century this area was a garden of Abul Fath Zadeh, now located in the modern village of Shah 'Abd al-Azim (partially built on the buried ruins of Rayy), but in earlier periods it had been a thriving residential neighborhood within the walls of the medieval city. However, archaeological context — the locations and relationships between artifacts that are found — builds a bridge that links ceramics to the setting where daily life occurred. Context can provide immediate answers to basic questions at Rayy, such as who used these ceramics, how they used them, and why they left them behind.

It is an intriguing fact that some of the most beautiful Islamic ceramics have been reassembled from broken fragments that people threw out as trash. People in pre-modern times had no garbage removal service, and the

View of excavations at Abul Fath Zadeh looking west

23

most convenient way to get rid of unwanted or broken objects was to bury them in pits beside their houses. Erich Schmidt, the director of the excavations, explains this finding in one of his unpublished preliminary reports:

> In the largest ... sounding a considerable part of a city block was uncovered, the entire area of more than 600 square meters being covered with remains of houses with their vaulted, semi-subterranean storerooms and innumerable refuse pits, as usual the "treasure boxes" of the excavation. The sterility of the rooms is as puzzling as the fertility of these sewage pits and wells which had been used as receptacles for broken and discarded vessels and other objects ... [supplying] the beautiful vessels of Abbasid and Saljuq times. – Schmidt, "Rayy Excavations – Season 1935"

The close connection between ceramics, refuse pits, and houses at Rayy suggests that ceramics played a very important role in domestic family life, as is the case in many cultures. Fired ceramics can be useful containers for all kinds of objects — food, liquids, money, or other valuables — and their relatively cheap manufacture adds to their appeal. If a ceramic vessel breaks, it is usually possible to throw it away and buy or make another, and this is exactly the reason why hundreds of thousands of ceramic sherds gradually built up in the trash pits of Rayy's neighborhoods. What is distinctive about Rayy, however, is the decoration and artistry of many of these sherds and vessels. At Islamic Rayy it was not only rulers, court life, and wealthy patrons who supported the arts. Ordinary families also invested in beauty in their private, daily lives.

The ways that decoration complemented and enhanced daily activities was extensive and can be seen in the many functions of ceramics found in the excavated neighborhood. One of the clearest roles of ceramics, however, was in connection with eating and drinking. Food and culture often go hand in hand, such as through communal eating which fosters social relationships or common religious proscriptions against certain foods. For example, many of Rayy's ceramics were used in a Persian culture of cuisine that reveled in the experience of dining and eventually became popular throughout the Islamic world. Persian foods were adopted by the Abbasid caliphate in Iraq and their recipes were spread to Egypt and beyond. At the same time, Islamic concepts of hospitality and dining were intertwined with Persian traditions of feasting to create a pan-Islamic culture of cuisine.

Any study needs to be careful not to over-simplify the shared aspects of culture, as it varies even within one place. Rayy, for example, was always a diverse society where various social and ethnic differences existed. However,

ERICH SCHMIDT'S ACCOUNT OF THE EXCAVATION OF THE NEIGHBORHOOD

Thus, once a crew of thirty laborers has been put to work in an excavation square of ten by ten meters, its members soon disappear individually in the numerous pits which are defined by loose, often greenish dirt. Such pits are sometimes as deep as twenty yards and many days are required to excavate them with small trowels. Once a certain part of the square and its pits are exhausted, the excavation level is carried somewhat deeper, and new pits appear, belonging as a rule, to a period slightly preceding the time during which the top pits had been dug. Again the crew disappears and a few men only with windlasses and screens for sifting the dirt are visible in the excavation area. In this manner, more than a month is required to exhaust any spot in Islamic Rayy.

— Schmidt, "Rayy Spring Season 1936"

the nature of the excavations at Rayy does not easily lend itself to an evaluation of these social relationships within the city. Only one residential neighborhood has been excavated, and it is therefore difficult to make any comparisons about whether the city was divided into ethnic neighborhoods or whether ceramics and cuisines were different depending on a family's social standing or background. For now, Rayy's ceramics should be viewed as a test case of society. They may not reflect the attitudes and values of all Rayy's residents, but hopefully they can still shed light on some of the most common aesthetics and values of both Persian and Islamic culture at Rayy.

Cooking in Medieval Persia

The thick clay walls of the vessel shown on the right (OIM A115123) would have prevented it from breaking while cooking food over a fire, and its purpose can be confirmed by the dark build up of soot on its base. Decoration had a place in cooking as well as eating. Undulating lines are incised along the edge of the rim of this vessel, and it probably originally had a cover that would also have been embellished with abstract designs.

Reconstructing what this bowl might have cooked is a much more difficult task since no Persian cooking manuals have survived from a similar period.[19] However, several famous medieval Arabic cookery books borrow directly from Persian recipes and provide an

Red earthenware bowl with incised decoration along edge of rim. OIM A115123

idea of what people might have been eating at Rayy. This bowl might have been used to make a brothy soup of chickpeas or a more hearty stew, rich with fruits like raisins or pomegranates and garnished with minced meat and spices such as coriander, cumin, pepper, cinnamon, and ginger. These dishes would have also included one of a variety of grains such as pasta (sometimes cooked in sour yogurt), rice (colored with saffron), or bread.[20]

Manuscript painting. 1560s, Qazvin, Iran. Ink, opaque pigments, and gold on paper. 28.5 x 19 cm. The David Collection, Copenhagen. 51/1980

It is almost impossible to determine from the ceramics of Rayy the gender or age of people who were doing the cooking, but it was probably a family affair. The houses near the pits where the ceramics were found were organized around private family life, a value that characterizes Islamic culture from Cairo to Istanbul and Samarqand. These homes did not directly face the street of the neighborhood; instead guests would first enter through the main door into a long passageway and then a private courtyard, around which all the rooms of the house faced. Rooms could be easily adapted to changing functions depending on seasonal weather, expansions of the family, or different storage needs.

Rim sherds of earthenware vessels with incised decoration. OIM A115056, A115061, A115057

The Culture of Cuisine

At first glance, the forms of ceramics from Rayy's trash pits might look like inconsequential fragments. Their long deposition in the ground has worn away some of their brilliant turquoise and green glazes and many of the pieces are rather small. It takes a careful eye to imagine the original vessels, but this process does lead to some interesting conclusions. For example, the shapes of the ceramics shown here indicate that they were used during the experience of dining.

After the Islamic conquest in the seventh century, Rayy (like many other Persian cities) was witness to a diverse population of ethnic groups, but common patterns of life emerged. The resulting culture combined a Muslim esteem for hospitality with indigenous Persian traditions. Some of the most famous sayings ascribed to the Islamic prophet Muhammad concern generosity with food: "The best among you is he who feeds people," "Eat together and do not separate. Blessing is in society."[21] Similarly, the pre-Islamic Persian court relished in elaborate conventions of social dining and food preparation which carried over into the Islamic period.

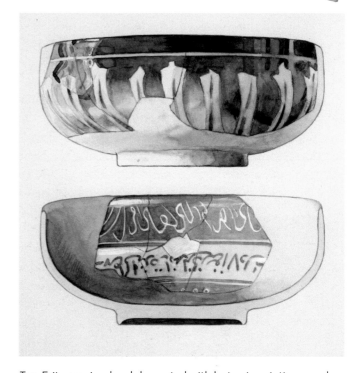

While elaborate feasting conventions were probably only used in a limited way in the non-royal neighborhoods of Rayy, ornamented ceramics show a true investment in the dining experience in these areas as well. The foods of the medieval Persian world, although widely varied, lacked the colors of New World vegetables. It is therefore likely that the vessels which framed a meal with a festive sense of design and decoration were some of the brightest colors in a dining experience.

Some of the most common ceramic vessels found in the excavations of the neighborhood are bowls of many different sizes. While styles of decoration seem to vary by period with little connection to function, the shapes of these bowls are much more informative about the culture of cuisine. Many foods (such as thick stews) would have been served in small bowls and eaten with the hand, a common tradition in Islamic cultures. Larger bowls were made for communal use.

Although these bowls require more research in order to determine the proportion of individual to communal vessels, the basic aspects of bowl use in medieval Islamic cities is already fairly well known. Medieval accounts relate

Top: Fritware rim sherd decorated with luster, inscription on edge of rim. OIM A115088
Bottom: Watercolor reconstruction of the complete vessel, artist unknown. Oriental Institute, RG 3320

that people dined while sitting on the floor, and the bowls from Rayy might have been laid on a thick cloth around which people gathered for the meal. Special bowls for serving nuts and sweetened fruit candies are also found at Rayy. Such appetizers were often presented during the long social preliminaries to a major meal, a custom that dates back to pre-Islamic Sasanian Persia and continued into the Islamic period.[22]

Left: Watercolor of a bowl with incised decoration under green glaze, artist unknown. Oriental Institute, RH 7445.
Right: Watercolor of a bowl with turquoise glaze, artist unknown. Oriental Institute, RCi 4021

Serving vessels for liquids are another common type of ceramic found in the neighborhood at Rayy. Many of these jugs, ewers, and cups probably held water as the typical complement to a meal. Rayy, with its numerous streams and flowing canals, was known for its abundant drinking water.[23] However, while Islam forbids the drinking of alcoholic beverages, Rayy was renowned for its barley beer, and its people also drank wines and milk. Alternatively, one of the more popular drinks may have been syrups derived from the juice of pomegranates, lemons, apricots, and other fruits.

Many Islamic serving vessels cleverly combine decoration and function. Some of the most creative designs draw on Iran's pre-Islamic heritage, such as ewers crafted with spouts that are shaped like the heads of animals, which are also found in pre-Islamic periods. The fragmentary example shown below (OIM A115067) was probably the head of a bull, light-heartedly designed so that wa-

Clockwise from top left: Base of fritware cup with turquoise glaze (OIM A115179); watercolor of jug with incised decoration under turquoise glaze, artist unknown (Oriental Institute, RH 4818); watercolor of fritware cup with molded decoration under turquoise glaze, artist unknown (Oriental Institute, RH 4578)

ter would pour from the mouth. Other serving vessels — even those without glaze — were also palettes for decorative experimentation. One of the most imaginative examples is this jug (OIM A115122) which has ripples of appliqué. These strands are complemented by sherd fragments of turquoise glazed vessels that have been pressed into the red clay around the neck, creating a playful accent of color.

Fritware ewer spout in the shape of an animal head; turquoise glaze. OIM A115067

Above: Rim and neck of earthenware jug inset with small glazed ceramic fragments. OIM A115059
Right: Red earthenware jug decorated in appliqué and inset with small glazed ceramic fragments. OIM A115122

FEASTING IN NIZAMI'S *HAFT PAYKAR*

Bahram Gur with the Tartar princess in the green pavilion. From a manuscript of Nizami's *Khamsa*, ca. 1580, Shiraz, Iran. Opaque watercolor and gold on paper, 15.5 x 10 in. Collection of the Art Institute of Chicago, Gift of Ann McNear. 1983.626

The poet Nizami, born at Ganja in the Caucasus in ca. 1140, was considered one of the greatest poets of romantic epic in Persian literature. His writings would have been well known at Rayy. One of his most popular works was the *Haft Paykar* (Seven Beauties), a romanticized account of the Sasanian king Bahram Gur. This story tells of Bahram Gur's quest to marry the seven most beautiful princesses from around the world. In order to attract the princesses, Bahram Gur builds seven beautiful pavilions of seven different colors. At their arrival, each princess tries to impress the king with a story expressing a different mood and moral. In the painting shown here, the Turkman princess tells her story to Bahram Gur under the dome of a brightly decorated green pavilion, while entertainers perform with music and dance.

The scene, although illustrated at a much later date than the ceramics of Rayy, is a window into the Persian custom of feasting on a grand ceremonial scale. It is rich with action and detail, drawing the eyes from one figure to the next and emphasizing the connection between hospitality, entertainment, and dining in the Persian world. The main figures recline on a large carpet, surrounded by attendants and other guests, and fine foods and drink are laid out around them.

The Fine Line between Decoration and Function

Some of the ceramics found in the neighborhoods of Rayy are so extensively decorated that it is easy to wonder if they were appreciated and displayed solely for their decoration rather than used to hold food. This bowl (RH 5590) displays detailed scenes of seated figures using a luster colored glaze, a technique that required high technical skill for successful firing and would have been much more expensive to produce than other glazes. Was it used daily during meals by a wealthy family who wanted to flaunt its status or was it cherished for special occasions by a person of more humble means? Objects like this bring up an important question — where does decoration stop and function begin, and vice versa?

In many ways, this question is unanswerable. Even in modern life a single object can have many functions, and we put objects to use in ways for which they were never originally intended. In studying the past, the problem of interpreting function is compounded, especially for ceramics, since they — and their decoration — could be so versatile. The difficulty of connecting decoration with function is the reason why extra information about findspots and the relationships between objects can be so important. Two examples in this

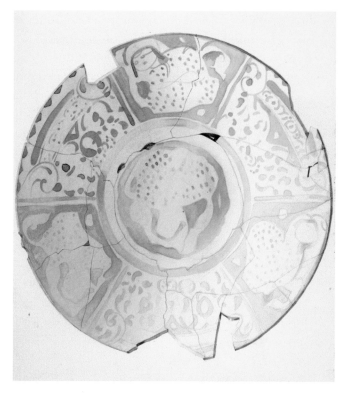

Watercolor of a fritware bowl painted in luster over opaque white glaze, artist unknown. Oriental Institute, RH 5590

exhibition — animal sculptures and the enigmatic "grenade" — show that both decoration and archaeological context play an important role in answering some of the most long-standing mysteries of Islamic ceramics.

This sculpture of an elephant (RH 6105) is crafted in the delicate style of twelfth-century Persian ceramics. The abstract representations of round shields on its ears and decorative blankets or protective armor along its body are wonderfully detailed and the *howdah* (railed platform) on its back may have originally seated small human figures. This sculpture was one of Schmidt's most exciting finds in the neighborhood excavations in 1935. He writes,

Watercolor of a ceramic elephant figurine; fritware with turquoise glaze, artist unknown. Oriental Institute, RH 6105

One of the most interesting ceramic master pieces is a large effigy vessel, or, rather, pottery sculpture. It is an elephant coated with a turquoise glaze. With infinite patience our head restorer succeeded to fit the pieces of this beautiful specimen which were scattered in many different pits and in the refuse of several rooms. Finally, about four-fifths of the unique specimen were assembled while the rest [was] restored in gypsum. — Schmidt, "Rayy Excavations – Season 1935"

Islamic sculptures of elephants, camels, bulls, and other animals are found in many museum collections of Islamic art, but modern knowledge of their function remains ambiguous since they often seem to be limited by the fragility of their decoration. Some examples have spouts as if they were meant to contain liquid or perfume, but impractical angles and thin handles suggest these are only a remnant form of decoration. The finest objects, such as the elephant figurine, probably had a ceremonial or commemorative importance, or were valued for their symbolism. Some figures of ceramic elephants may have been symbols of royal power because of their role carrying princely personages in court processions and in warfare, a tradition originating in India.[24] However, this elephant was probably used and broken in a domestic context and may have been considered more of an auspicious symbol for the home instead of a royal one.

Base and legs of a bull figurine; fritware with blue glaze. OIM A115161, A115162

Smaller, less decorative animal figures, such as these fragments of a bull (OIM A115161, A115162), probably had a more functional use. Its base is unglazed and might have been used as a soothing scrubbing platform during a visit to the bath,[25] an important aspect of urban life throughout the Islamic world. This use is not entirely certain, and an alternative view is that the figure might have functioned as a small vessel, holding perfume or rose water.

The exact function of a type of small, round vessel shown to the right has puzzled Islamic scholars for over a hundred years, and debate continues today. Most publications now call them sphero-conical vessels in reference to their shape. They are surprisingly heavy and almost as hard as rock since they were fired with an especially dense clay mixture. They are found at archaeological sites throughout the wide arc of the Islamic world, therefore they must have been well known and had a special function. Originally, scholars thought that these objects were hand grenades, meant to shatter on impact to spill their contents of "Greek fire" (*naphtha*) in war. However, this dramatic image of Islamic warfare also came with a tinge of doubt. If these vessels were meant to break easily, shouldn't they be much thinner? Although the two examples shown here are fragmentary, large numbers of this type of vessel have been found whole at other archaeological sites. In addition, if they were made only to be destroyed, why were they typically given so much decoration?

Archaeological context has provided scholars with an even clearer answer why these curious vessels were not grenades and has helped to suggest some more likely functions. Similar to findings at other sites, many of Rayy's sphero-conical vessels were discovered in private houses and domestic areas, tossed into refuse pits with other ceramic bowls and jars. Obviously, they were objects of daily life. From this information, some scholars propose that they stored mercury, which in the medieval period was commonly used as a medicinal drug for the (probably unsuc-

Rims and shoulders of two sphero-conical vessels. OIM A115053, A115054

cessful) treatment of a variety of illnesses.[26] However, hundreds of these vessels have been found throughout the Middle East — dozens came from the limited excavations of Rayy — and mercury was too rare to have filled them all. Other scholars suggest they were aeolipiles to be filled with water and placed on a fire to add moisture to the air,[27] or bottles containing a fizzy beer drink that had to be tightly covered,[28] or even a part of water-pipes used for smoking.[29] Having all of these hypotheses is not a negative aspect; it is completely possible that sphero-conical vessels had multiple functions, just like other types of pottery.

Still, there is always an unspoken aim in scholarly circles to classify, to find the most likely function, and decoration can provide additional clues about sphero-conical vessels. Many of them have small protruding knobs of clay called "prunts" attached to the sides, which would have made them easier to hold. Even more remarkably, some of these vessels have inscriptions, almost like modern food labels. Two examples from the art market that are said to have been found at Rayy are inscribed with short phrases in Arabic: "drink to your good health" and "divine grace to its owner, drink, made by Hamshad."[30] Although the excavated vessels depicted here do not have full inscriptions, two of those found at Rayy are stamped with the word *baqi*, which is related to the English word "remainder." Some scholars have argued that this was the name of either the potter or the owner. However, the presence of a similar inscription on a similar vessel made in Hama (Syria) suggests that it might have been a reference to the contents of the vessel,[31] or possibly even a type of measurement.

LINKS TO A WIDER WORLD

At Rayy, the popularity of ceramic styles waxed and waned as new technologies and designs were developed. Analyzing these changes does not simply result in a list of typologies stating sizes, designs, and rim styles. The changes in style unmistakably show that Rayy was connected to a wider Islamic culture that shared in similar patterns of lifestyle. In fact, Islamic culture can be defined by the remarkable ease of travel, trade, and exchange that facilitated common development of ideas and technologies during the medieval period.

Anyone approaching the medieval culture of Rayy for the first time takes on the daunting task of negotiating the complexities of Middle Eastern history. Rayy was occupied by a multitude of dynasties, governors, and conquerors — a consequence of the constantly shifting political fortunes of northern Iran during this period. Governments that spanned the Middle East like the Umayyad caliphate (661–750) and the Abbasid caliphate (750–1258) are better known, but other groups at Rayy such as the Samanids, Buyids, Ghaznawids, and Ghuzz are unfamiliar to most people. Many of these dynasties ruled as proxies of the Abbasids but were actually fairly independent and preoccupied with complex local power struggles. It can be a challenge to see their relevance to the wider scope of history.

In the case of Rayy, these groups do not even appear to form a cohesive society or period. They represent a chain of different ethnic backgrounds — including groups with Persian, Arab, and Turkic origins — a sign of the migrations of populations moving through northern Iran during this time. While these dynasties all endorsed the religion of Islam, even this does not always indicate unity in the region since they variously promoted Sunni or Shi'ite forms, a theological divide which then as now could serve as a source of tension. How can we call this one period, or one culture? At an even more fundamental level, what is the foundation of a shared Islamic culture?

In the material culture of Rayy it is possible to see common ways of living. As an example, similar forms and decorative traditions of ceramics were used throughout Rayy, and also over much of Iran and beyond. They are an indication of a common Islamic culture at Rayy not fundamentally based on politics but still reliant on close contacts between people. In the Islamic period these contacts often seem to be closely related to a revitalization of physical routes of travel and trade. Rayy was wide open to these influences due to its geographic location at the crossroads of two major highways through Iran. From west to east, the great Khurasan road passed through Rayy as it crossed from Anatolia and Mesopotamia into Central Asia and China. This route is better known as one of the most traveled of the Silk Roads, part of a loose network of routes through Eurasia that fostered cultural exchanges between the world's earliest civilizations. Rayy also held a strategic position along a north–south axis of trade through Iran, connecting Azerbaijan in the north to Isfahan and the Persian Gulf. Archaeology can help explain and document Rayy's role in this network through comparisons of the material culture at different points along its paths, and through an exploration of which cities and sites have the closest relationships.

Ultimately, Rayy's ceramics do more than confirm the city's important role as an economic crossroads. They also show that Rayy's connection to the rest of the Islamic world was deeper than trade since trade was complemented by a common development of technology, symbolism, and tradition. Even more importantly, Rayy's role in a wider Islamic world was also continually changing. These cultural links were not particularly dependent on changes in political control, except in the ways that politics altered economic conditions. Rayy's ceramics show that these connections could also extend in unexpected and far-reaching ways, helping to define the real boundaries of Islamic culture.

THE TRAVELS OF AL-MUQADDASI

Political histories are only one part of a large body of historical writings — including travel accounts, geographies, memoirs, and social commentaries — and some of these documents address culture very directly. Combining evidence from these sources along with archaeological data is a useful comparative method for understanding culture at Rayy. One of the most fascinating descriptions of medieval Rayy was written by al-Muqaddasi, a tenth-century scholar who traveled extensively throughout the Middle East and compiled his journey into a detailed geography of the Islamic world. He apparently believed in the poetic balance of praise with negative comments; his descriptions both extol the wonders of Rayy and convey a sense of his personal experiences and trials during his stay there:

> Al-Rayy is an important town, delightful, distinguished; many glories and much fruit; the markets are spacious, the hostels, attractive, the baths good, foods aplenty, little to hurt one, abundance of water, flourishing commerce. Learned people are the leaders, the public is intelligent, the women are good housekeepers; the stores are splendid. The weather is pleasing; it is an elegant, clean place... Here are councils and schools; natural talents, handicrafts; granaries... Here is a library of remarkable books; the amazing "courtyard of the watermelon," the delightful al-Rudha. Here is a castle, and an inner city... In fact, al-Rayy is beyond what we have described; however, its water causes diarrhea, its melons kill... There is little firewood, much discord. Their meats are hard, their hearts are hard, their congregation disagreeable. The Imams at the mosque are at variance, one day for the Hanafites, one day for the Shafi'ites.

> — al-Muqaddasi, *Best Divisions for Knowledge*, p. 347

Where Are the Umayyads? (SEVENTH AND EIGHTH CENTURIES)

Daily Life Ornamented covers a range of six centuries of ceramics at Rayy, from the ninth through the fourteenth centuries. Those with some background in Islamic history may notice that there is a significant discrepancy between these dates and traditional starting point of Islamic history in the seventh century, which leaves out two centuries of Islamic life at Rayy. Of course, these early years are not intentionally omitted, but the gap occurs because very few ceramics from this collection can be securely dated to the beginning of the Islamic era. This problem is characteristic of almost all Iranian collections of Islamic ceramics.

Early Islamic ceramics are probably not really "missing" from Rayy's collection but rather are simply difficult to recognize, some having likely been misidentified as pre-Islamic material during the original excavations. Early Islamic ceramics represent a transitional period when Iran shifted from an independent political center under the Sasanians into a district of a large inter-regional Islamic realm under the Umayyad caliphate. The caliphate was a governmental system that developed soon after the death of Muhammad in 632, when Arabian political elites took control of large sections of the Middle East. By the early 700s, the world of Islam stretched from North Africa to the edge of India.

Arab power was consolidated in Rayy at an early stage in this process of conquest, between 639 and 644, but local patterns of Iranian life persisted for many years, including the types of ceramics people used. The area of Rayy was administered by governors of the Umayyad dynasty, who were based in the capital city of Damascus in distant Syria, but popular styles and influence from this western center do not seem to have become popular at Rayy. Even the adoption of the new religion of Islam was gradual, and conversion took place very slowly over generations.[32] It is only after the passing of power from the Umayyads to the Abbasids that Rayy's connection to the wider Islamic world becomes clear in its material culture.

Another possibility for why early Islamic ceramics are lacking is because glazing technology was not as widely used in this period, and unglazed objects have not received as much study as more beautifully decorated types. Early Islamic ceramics probably do exist in the Rayy collection, but these undecorated pots are difficult to distinguish without a full knowledge of the stratigraphy of the pits where they were found, which helps to date them. This information was collected but still needs to be analyzed and will be available once a full archaeological report of the site is conducted. At present, our knowledge is limited to Schmidt's very preliminary discussion of ceramics from the early Islamic levels at Rayy:

> [There are] sparsely sprinkled chips of turquoise glaze on plain pitcher necks, but otherwise glazed ceramics were totally absent in the lowest Islamic levels. – Schmidt, "Rayy Expedition Report II – August 1934"

> The early Islamic plain ware is far more elegant and variegated than the unglazed ceramics of Middle Islam. One of the characteristic features of the earlier plain ware consists of faint indentation encircling in oblique rows the bodies of jars and pitchers. – Schmidt, "Rayy Excavations – Season 1935"

The Abbasids and Their Proxies at Rayy (NINTH TO ELEVENTH CENTURIES)

Rayy's ceramics reveal much more about Islamic culture during the Abbasid period. The Abbasid dynasty had close links to the Persian world. When they claimed the caliphate from the Umayyads in 749/750, they moved the capital from Damascus to Baghdad in Iraq, a better geographic center for rule over an expanded Islamic world. The politics of Abbasid rule at Rayy can be seen as a period of conflicting motivations. At times it was a golden age of prosperity and magnificent royal courts, which ultimately inspired some of the famous tales of Scheherazade in The Book of One Thousand and One Nights. The most famous Abbasid caliph, Harun al-Rashid (763-809), was born

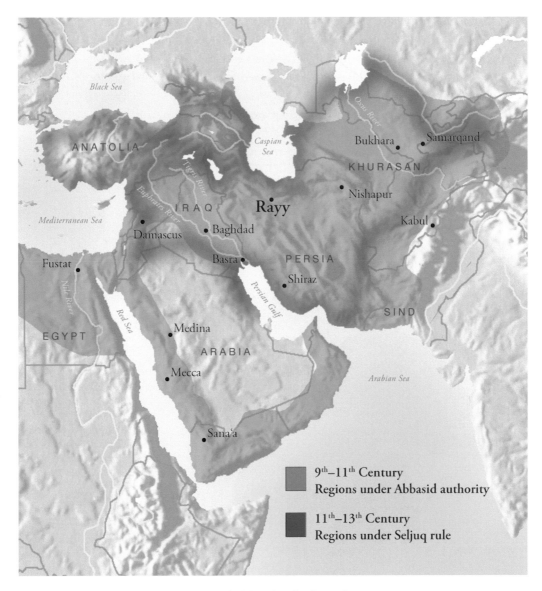

Map of Abbasid and Seljuq rule

at Rayy, and although he ruled from Baghdad and other cities, he continued to return to Rayy throughout his life. One of his visits, in 804/805, has been particularly memorialized as an example of his justice and good rule since he came to investigate complaints against the regional governor.

However, this same story also hints at a troubling succession of government officials at Rayy. This pattern ultimately devolved into struggles between small ancillary governments that were only nominally loyal to the Abbasids. Harun al-Rashid's own sons fought a civil war outside the gates of Rayy for control of the empire.[33] More clashes between the Daylamis and the Samanids were to follow in the coming years (912–925), and later between the Buyids and the Ghaznavids (925–1035), until the Seljuq Turks took control of the city in 1042.

The roller coaster of political fortune was a reality at Rayy, but it was only one aspect of a larger experience of life in the city. This same period was also witness to a distinctive synthesis of Rayy's material culture, which fully integrated Islamic traditions of the Arab conquerors, an indigenous Persian heritage, and new trade contacts with the Far East. This process can be clearly seen in innovations of ceramic technology with the introduction of new shapes, new glazes, and new designs. Ceramics at Rayy in particular combine traditions from the western areas of the Islamic world and eastern regions, indicating Rayy's special geographical role in the growth of a common Islamic culture. The ceramics on exhibit are just a few examples from the many different types of ceramics found at Rayy from this period, but they are some of the most revealing examples of Rayy's place in a wider world.

Glossy green and turquoise glazes are one of the longest-lasting traditions of ceramic decoration in the Middle East, a technique that adds iron and copper to an alkaline glaze to create strong, solid colors. Potters produced these wares in the Sasanian and Parthian periods. Many of Rayy's simple, functional bowls from the Islamic period continue these techniques. However, the Islamic period is notable for the development of multi-colored ceramic glazes that present a significant departure from the solid blue and green-glazed ceramics of pre-Islamic Persia.

The watercolors at the right show some of the earliest examples of the new palette of colors at Islamic Rayy, expanded from green to include yellows, browns, and purples. The designs were created with several glazing techniques. Some colored glazes were painted directly onto the clay, but in the case of the *albarello* (cylindrical jar) here (RH 4796), the outside of the vessel was first coated with a light-colored clay, called a slip, to make a white backdrop for the colored stripes.

Above: Watercolor of bowl with green splash decoration over opaque white glaze, artist unknown (Oriental Institute, RE 3135). *Below:* Watercolor of earthenware *albarello* with slip-painting under polychrome glaze, artist unknown (Oriental Institute, RH 4796)

Clockwise from top left: Rim of earthenware bowl with polychrome glaze (OIM A115003); base of earthenware vessel with polychrome glaze (OIM A115131); rim of earthenware bowl with slip-painted decoration (OIM A115098); rim of earthenware bowl with slip-painted decoration (OIM A115099); fragment of earthenware bowl with splash decoration in brown glaze (OIM A115104)

The simple designs of radiating stripes and dots used in conjunction with these colors are not found only at Rayy. This style was much more common in Egypt, Arabia, and Syria, where similar examples are called "Fayyoumi wares" or "Hijazi wares." Research is only just beginning to shed light on the widespread use of these polychrome ceramics, and at present little is known about how this technique spread through the Middle East. Polychrome ceramics seem to have had many centers of manufacture.[34] These examples were likely made at Rayy, while the technical details of their manufacture were widely exchanged.

White-glazed sherds with decorations of green and cobalt are also part of a fascinating story of trade and transmission that is typical of the early Islamic world. Rayy's examples contain only the faint remnants of the original colored designs, so it takes imagination to visualize their original appearance. However, they are our most important evidence for the reach of international trade in the Abbasid period. These sherds (OIM A115129, A115145, A115144) were once part of opaque whiteware bowls with rounded sides and a curving flare at the rim, a form which was copied from Chinese whitewares imported into the Middle East. Although many people might assume that Chinese ceramics were traded along the Silk Roads, the richest findings of luxury Chinese ceramics have been found at archaeological sites along the ports of the Persian Gulf. These indicate that Islamic markets may have first been supplied by maritime rather than land trade with China.[35] One might imagine a parade of boats loaded with trade wares circling the Indian Ocean year-round through Africa, the Middle East, and Asia, taking advantage of seasonal monsoon winds to complete their long journeys.

Clockwise from top left: Earthenware rim sherd with opaque white glaze and decoration in blue (OIM A115129); earthenware rim sherd with opaque white glaze and decoration in turquoise (OIM A115145); earthenware sherd with opaque white glaze and decoration in turquoise and blue (OIM A115144)

Islamic potters and their patrons must have greatly admired Chinese porcelain, as they both copied and elaborated on these prototypes to create a wide market based on this style. The fine kaolin clay used for the white-bodied fabric of Chinese porcelain was unavailable in the Middle East, so Islamic potters devised alternative techniques to achieve a smooth, white surface over local clay bodies. They formulated a new recipe for an opaque white glaze (usually made with tin oxides) that completely covered the reddish brown color of the underlying clay. Although Chinese porcelains rarely had colored designs, Islamic opaque whitewares were decorated in a distinctly new aesthetic of restrained flourishes of blue, sweeping lines of turquoise, and even phrases of Arabic inscriptions.

Scholars once thought that this type of ware was only produced in Iraq (with a main center of production at Basra), under the sponsorship of Abbasid political elites, and then distributed to markets across the Iranian plateau by donkey or camel. Recently, however, archaeological finds of opaque whitewares show regional specialties of manufacture coming from a variety of sites: Nishapur in northeast Iran, Siraf along the Persian Gulf, Samarra on the Euphrates River in Iraq, Fustat in Egypt, and Rayy in the middle of this activity.[36] Although these centers had different political orientations, their production of Islamic opaque wares show that they were all connected by common developments of industry, a sign that the Islamic world was connected by shared attitudes and not just superficial trading exchanges.

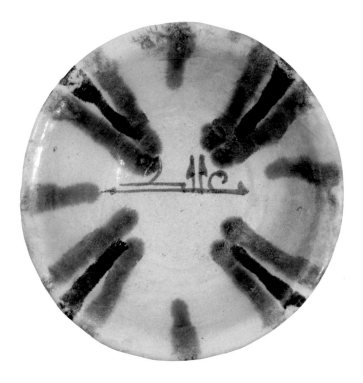

Bowl. The David Collection, Copenhagen. 38/2001

Rayy had connections not only to the southern coasts of the Islamic world, but also along the northern arc of the Silk Roads that led toward Central Asia, where styles of slip-painted ceramics and sgraffiato wares were popular in the Abbasid period. Slip wares were decorated with thin coats of different colored clays instead of glazes. They were manufactured in the eastern Khurasan province of Iran in cities such as Nishapur and Samarqand. Only a few slip-painted wares were found in the excavations of Rayy, which suggests that these ceramics were not made by Rayy's potters; they were probably imported into Rayy from eastern centers such as Nishapur.

Rayy's sgraffiato wares, with bold designs incised into the clay surface, are a better indication of the growth of a common Islamic tradition of material culture oriented around the Silk Roads. This type of ceramic, especially those examples with incised designs accented by colored glazes of greens, yellows, and manganese purple, have been found in excavations across northern Iran and also into Iraq and Anatolia. The popularity of sgraffiato wares took hold in these areas by the tenth century,[37] but within the next few centuries they also spread throughout the Islamic world, west into the Levant and eventually south into Egypt.

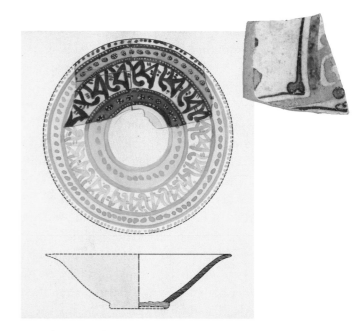

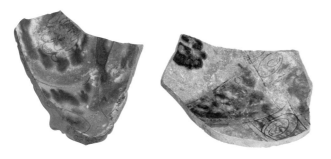

Top: Base of earthenware bowl with incised decoration under a polychrome glaze (OIM A115002).
Bottom: Base of earthenware bowl with incised decoration under a polychrome glaze (OIM A115128)

Earthenware sherd with slip-painted decoration (OIM A115146); watercolor reconstruction of the earthenware bowl from which it came, artist unknown. Oriental Institute, N47 1/2

The Turkic Migrations (ELEVENTH TO THIRTEENTH CENTURIES)

As early as the ninth century, during Abbasid rule, large numbers of Turkic-speaking slaves from Central Asia were conscripted into the various armies of the Islamic world. In the eleventh century, a more fundamental societal shift occurred with the migration of entire groups of Turks into central Iran and Anatolia. Rayy's position along a major route of travel through Iran made it vulnerable to these incursions, and in 1042 it fell to a Turkic dynasty known as the Seljuqs. During the next two centuries, Rayy became one of the principle cities of a large Seljuq empire.

There are conflicting views on the fate of economic prosperity during Seljuq rule in Iran, and it has generally been seen as an era that continued the fragmentation of the late Abbasid period.[38] Although the Seljuqs ruled over a vast region that included much of modern-day Iran, Iraq, Syria, and Anatolia, the realm was divided between different members of the Seljuq family who governed autonomously with varying levels of success. The Seljuqs also awarded salaries to members of the court and the army in the form of land grants (*iqta'*). Since these land grants frequently changed ownership, long-term investment in agriculture dwindled, weakening the economy and causing many peasants to flee to the cities.[39] New taxes were also imposed and several industries became government monopolies. Surprisingly, despite the disjointed state of the economy, archaeological finds show that the ceramic market in Iran continued to thrive, even experiencing a jolt of creativity and a diffusion of new technology, indicating an unexpected prosperity in cosmopolitan life in Seljuq cities such as Rayy.

Left to right: Rim of fritware bowl with transparent glaze (OIM A115154); earthenware rim sherd with white slip and incised decoration under transparent glaze, green pigment along edge (OIM A115022); fragment of fritware bowl with blue decoration under transparent glaze (OIM A115065); watercolor of fritware bowl with blue decoration under transparent glaze, artist unknown (Oriental Institute, RH 5548)

Potters of the Seljuq period took advantage of a completely new form of technology — fritware — to craft thin-bodied luxury ceramics inspired by incised Chinese porcelain and fine metalwork vessels.[40] Fritware is a mixture of ground quartz and a small amount of fine clay. It is a very flexible medium that can be worked into more elaborate shapes than pure clay. In the Islamic era, fritware was used for both simple but elegant utilitarian vessels, as well as a base for some of the most elaborate ceramic masterpieces of the period. These often employed complex glazing techniques and firing technologies. Most of the fritware vessels shown above (OIM A115065, A115154, A115022, RH 5548) are standard products of the Seljuq ceramic industry, decorated with a clear glaze that brings out the pure white color of the fritware body. Others have a strong turquoise glaze that over the following centuries became one of the most dominant colors of Iranian ceramics.

Along with continuing traditions of earthenwares, such as the incised example here with a central medallion figure of a bird (RH 5179), the new market in fritware ceramics was embraced by Rayy's residents (and also eagerly excavated in relatively large quantities during the Rayy expedition). Fritwares were a relatively cheap alternative to expensive foreign ceramics or precious metals, and as such their popularity seems to have been a response to a growing middle-class population in Seljuq Rayy, possibly contradicting the idea of economic stagnation in that period. In addition, the development of fritware can be called a pan-Islamic phenomenon since its popularity quickly spread between Egypt, Syria, and Iran. The conditions that promoted the spread of fritware technology throughout the Islamic world are complex, and Rayy's particular role in this process is explored further in the technology section of this catalogue.

There is less documentation for trade of Chinese goods for the Seljuq period of Iran than for the earlier Abbasid period, but extensive trade connections may be assumed to continue. The many imitations of Chinese porcelain at Rayy — both with fritware bodies and with decoration — indicate the continued popularity of Chinese ceramics in Middle Eastern markets. In fact, the sherds here with olive-green glaze and finely incised floral designs are from Chinese vessels that were likely imported into Rayy. The parallel to Rayy's native fritwares is quite obvious in the similarity of floral panels directly below the rims, which would have continued around the entire inside of a bowl.

Watercolor of earthenware bowl with white slip and incised decoration under a transparent glaze, green pigment around rim, artist unknown.
Oriental Institute, RH 5179

Clockwise from top left: Fritware sherd with incised decoration under green glaze (OIM A115167); fritware rim sherd with incised decoration under blue glaze (OIM A115085); Chinese celadon sherd with incised decoration under light green glaze (OIM A115013); fritware rim sherd with incised decoration under turquoise glaze (OIM A115166)

Rayy after the Mongols (FOURTEENTH CENTURY)

While the Mongol conquest of Persia in the mid-thirteenth century temporarily interrupted the area's prosperity, artisans soon recovered and expanded their trades under the "Pax Mongolica," a period of peace uniting parts of the Middle East, Central Asia, and China under the Mongol empire. However, this rejuvenation seems to have had less effect on Rayy, which literally drops out of most historical records after the Mongol conquest. This silence leaves us guessing what happened to Rayy's people during this time: Did they leave the city? Were they all killed during the invasion?

History and archaeology become complementary forms of evidence in trying to solve this mystery. Yaqut, an Arab scholar who fled across Iran before the armies of Genghis Khan, passed through Rayy in 1220–21 before the Mongols' arrival and recorded that most of the town was already in ruins.[41] Apparently, Rayy had succumbed to civil strife between Muslim religious factions in the early thirteenth century, which may have decimated the population of most of the city. Other accounts confirm that the surviving population of Rayy was massacred by the Mongols after they occupied the city in 1220. These accounts may be exaggerations of the devastation motivated by a general panic throughout the Middle East,[42] but archaeology confirms that much of the city was abandoned in the thirteenth century. Ceramics found at other archaeological sites from the early Mongol period (such as Sultanabad wares and *lajvardina* wares) are completely absent in the Oriental Institute's collection of Rayy's ceramics.

However, Rayy's ceramics also show that total abandonment is too simple an explanation, since the excavations found many ceramics which date to the fourteenth century and possibly beyond. Many of these later ceramics come from excavations of the Citadel mound. In an important correlation, historical documents mention that the citadel of Rayy was rebuilt under Ghazan Khan (1295–1304), the seventh Mongol ruler of the Iranian region. Rayy's ceramics help to confirm this revival and they are also evidence that Rayy was more than a short-term stop as military outpost. People must have actually settled and lived on the Citadel mound, rather than simply passing through on military campaigns, since ceramics continued to be manufactured, used, and thrown away in fairly large numbers.[43] Based on the types of ceramics found at the citadel, this settlement was probably limited to the fourteenth century. An Italian diplomat passing through the area in 1404 remarked that the old city of Rayy was no longer occupied.[44] However, settlement in the area continued outside the city walls in several nearby villages.

The citadel's ceramics show that Rayy's connections to the surrounding Islamic world were fundamentally altered during the Mongol period. The underglaze-painted wares of this period still share designs with ceramic markets to the west (Syria, Egypt), as had occurred in earlier periods, but these ceramics show a re-orientation toward the trends of the East and reflect Iran's new place in an eastern Islamic empire, the Mongol Ilkhanate.

Clockwise from left: Base of earthenware vessel with white slip, painted in black under transparent turquoise glaze (OIM A115194); base of fritware vessel painted blue and green under transparent glaze (OIM A115189); base of fritware vessel painted blue under transparent glaze (OIM A115084); fritware fragment, blue and green stripes on white interior (OIM A115190); fritware sherd with white slip painted black under transparent turquoise glaze (OIM A115184)

Rayy's underglaze-painted ceramics accentuate the major changes in available resources which occurred during the Ilkhanate re-occupation of Rayy. These ceramics no longer have fritware bodies but are formed from thickly potted clay. Fritware continued to be used throughout Iran during this period, and its absence at Rayy confirms that Rayy was no longer the glorious city of previous centuries and that it no longer had a market for luxury wares. Nevertheless, some of the ceramics shown here must have been greatly valued by the people who used them. This dish (OIM A115093, A115094, A115187) has holes drilled through the edges of each sherd so that the pieces could be tied together. Repairs such as this only happened if the dish was broken but considered too valuable or useful to throw away.

Fragment of earthenware dish with white slip, black and turquoise painted decoration under transparent glaze (OIM 115093, A115094, A115187)

Although the city of Rayy lost status during the Mongol period, its ceramics revive some of the styles of pre-Mongol Iran, indicating that Rayy was still influenced by its Islamic past. Underglaze painting of ceramics was used in the centuries before the Mongols, as was turquoise glaze with black abstract decorations and compartmentalizaton of designs on bowls using radiating panels.

Mongol period ceramic types, such as those found at Rayy, seem to have been used at a number of Iranian provincial centers but have received very little modern study.[45] Since underglaze-painted ceramics have such a firm connection to Rayy, they can provide a needed point of reference for future studies on the industry of these wares.

In addition to echoes of earlier traditions, some of Rayy's Citadel ceramics imitate the designs of Chinese Yuan blue-and-white porcelain of the fourteenth century. While the porcelain sherd below (OIM A115188) likely dates to the fourteenth century, the other examples shown (OIM A115191 and unlabeled watercolor) may be from later periods. The Mongol empire extended along the entirety of the Silk Road trade routes, so Rayy's link to this eastern source of decoration is understandable, even if Rayy was only a shadow of a city in this period. The Mongol period also brought a resurgence of large-scale oceanic trade between China, India, and the Islamic world,[46] which could have brought exposure to blue-and-white wares from an alternate direction through the Persian Gulf.

Rim of vessel, porcelain with blue and white glaze (OIM A115188)

Base of fritware vessel painted in blue and black under transparent glaze (OIM A115191)

Watercolor of bowl with underglaze painting, artist unknown. Oriental Institute. Unlabeled

RELIGIOUS INSPIRATIONS

At medieval Rayy, cultural values would have been expressed in many media — including literature, architecture, textiles, and metalwork — but many of these art forms are susceptible to deterioration and have not survived into the modern period. For example, the remarkable libraries mentioned by al-Muqaddasi at Rayy were lost early when the city was seized by Mahmud of Ghaza in 1042, making Rayy for a short while part of his expanding Afghan empire. Mahmud was a great patron of Persian literature and his armies carried off most of Rayy's books in one hundred loads to his capital in the east.

Other materials have been lost through more natural processes, such as the disintegration of textiles and other organic materials. Ceramics help to fill this stark gap in our knowledge of Rayy because they preserve the decorative conventions of Islamic life. Neither sherds nor whole vessels can ever provide a complete inventory of cultural meaning from these decorations, but they can help pinpoint some of the most significant influences that shaped Islamic culture.

Perhaps the most basic inspiration for the decoration of Rayy's ceramics is the religion of Islam. Very few ceramics are innately religious objects since they were used mainly in private residences for storage, cooking, and other secular activities. The people who used them may not have even practiced Islam; they might have been adherents to one of several different religions that existed in the Middle East during the medieval period, including Christianity, Judaism, and Zoroastrianism. Each of these religions had a cultural impact at Rayy, but the city's ceramics primarily resonate with the principles of Islam, the religion of a growing majority of the population.

The Islamic world is more naturally unified by the practice of Islam than by any geographic cohesion. Islam is a monotheistic religion that has the same Abrahamic roots as Christianity and Judaism. It is based on the holy book of the *Qur'an* (literally, "reading" or "recitation"). For Muslims, the Qur'an is a miracle of God which was revealed to the prophet Muhammad via the angel Gabriel in the seventh century. The core message of the Qur'an is the indivisible nature of God (*Allah* in Arabic) and an emphatic condemnation of idolatry. The Qur'an was initially passed down orally in Arabic from the Prophet to his followers and later written down in one complete book.

In contrast to Christianity, Islam makes less of a distinction between the religious and the secular aspects of life. For Muslims, the practice of "Islam," which literally means submission to the will of God, occurs at every moment of the day and can embrace all earthy matters. In this way, many secular ceramics can be seen as an extension of a religious world view, a reminder that every part of life is holy and harmonizes with the principles of religion.[47] The visual conventions of ceramic decoration can incorporate or promote religious values directly, as with religious inscriptions, but they more often resonate with the principles of Islam indirectly, as with the prominence of calligraphy and abstract designs.

Of course, because of the diversity of population at Rayy it is not reasonable to assume that all decorative motifs in Rayy's ceramics have religious inspirations, or that there is only one meaning. One of the most obvious discrepancies is with depiction of figures, a practice not encouraged by Islam. However, the principles of Islam still had a role in restricting the appropriate contexts for these types of ornament.

Questions about the inspirations of decoration are typically approached through the discipline of art history but this process is also shared with archaeologists. The ability to relate a ceramic to an archaeological context is an invaluable source of information because it shows that despite the ways that religion reverberated into all aspects of life, separate religious and secular contexts often existed. Mosques and other religious buildings echo religious values more closely, but ceramics found in domestic residences can also have inspirations from a variety of sources beyond religion.

Calligraphy: The Signature of Islamic Culture

Calligraphy decorates only a small proportion of the vast numbers of Islamic ceramics found in the excavations at Rayy, but these examples come from all periods of settlement at the city. Beautiful writing was consistently popular throughout the Islamic period. Persian, a language with Indo-European roots, was the dominant language of Iran during the Islamic period (as it continues to be in modern Iran) and some of the ceramics from Rayy bear

Persian inscriptions. Surprisingly though, many more are inscribed in the Arabic language or with multiple sections of text in both Persian and Arabic.

The popularity of Arabic as a form of decoration at Rayy, far from the language's roots in the northern region of the Arabian peninsula, came from the close association between calligraphy and the religion of Islam. Arabic was first introduced into Persia along with Islam by the Arabian political elites who administered the early Islamic empire, and government documents were often written with a simple cursive, or *naskhi*, script of written Arabic.[48] However, refined forms of calligraphy were created in order to reflect the special nature of important texts, and for Muslims, no text was more revered than the Qur'an. Since the text of the Qur'an was considered to be the actual words of God that were delivered to Muhammad in Arabic, it was important to preserve and honor every nuance. The Qur'an could not be translated; it was always written in Arabic, and Islamic calligraphy developed to enhance the specific linguistic properties of the Arabic language.

Arabic is a Semitic language which is based on groups of phonetic consonants that make up words, with changing vowel patterns which alter meaning. It is always written in a cursive script from right to left, with vowels added as dashes or dots above and below the main line of consonants. Fluent speakers of Arabic are able to read a text even if the vowels are omitted,

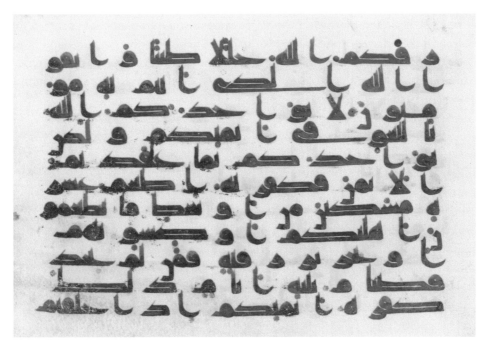

Clockwise from top left: Fritware sherd painted in black under a transparent turquoise glaze, inscription (OIM A15220); earthenware sherd with polychrome glaze, inscription (OIM A115138); cream earthenware sherd with molded decoration (OIM A115045); fritware sherd decorated with *minai* technique over opaque white glaze (OIM A115027)

as often occurs in the simplified inscriptions on ceramics. Most Qur'anic manuscripts, however, such as the example below (1982.1302), are more fully voweled. The contrast between long vertical upstrokes, the horizontal lengthening of letters, and the carefully positioned red vowel marks creates a rhythmic pattern that echoes the flow of spiritual imagery contained in the words. This style of calligraphy is called *kufic*, a name derived from an early Islamic settlement in

Leaf from the Qur'an. Sura al-Maida (The Repast), verses 88 and part of 89. Ninth/tenth century, North Africa or Near East. Black ink on vellum with red accents. 15.5 x 23.3 cm. Collection of the Art Institute of Chicago, Gift of Ann McNear. 1982.1302

southern Iraq called Kufa, but the term stands for a large family of calligraphic scripts of Arabic used for religious writings throughout the Middle East.[49] Rayy's ceramics include examples of the bold, angular kufic script as well as later forms of calligraphy that originated in Persia and have a more rolling, fluid movement.

The early expansion of the Islamic world was mainly political, and no populations were forced to convert to Islam. Conversion seems to have occurred very gradually over the following centuries, and the formal grandeur of Arabic calligraphy used in the early periods may have been limited to monumental inscriptions of government buildings and manuscripts sponsored by the royal court. Still, as the Muslim population expanded in the medieval period, Islamic principles also became an important source of inspiration for poets and artists in genres outside traditional Qur'anic manuscript making, such as in ceramics.

Fritware rim sherd luster painted over opaque white glaze. OIM A115019

Fritware rim sherd decorated in *minai* technique over opaque white glaze, front and back. OIM A115010

Ceramics were not usually considered appropriate for the holy character of full Qur'anic verses since they were used mainly in secular contexts, but they often drew from the ideology of the Qur'an. Although the script of these ceramic sherds is often difficult to read, some are ornamented with a religious blessing or the simple, repeating motif of one of God's names. One of the sherds above (OIM A115010, front) reads *al-iqbaal* "prosperity," a common formula in inscriptions of good wishes. The others have repeated names, *al-ghaalib* "the triumphant/victorious" (OIM A115010, back) and *al-haqq* "the just/the truth" (OIM A115019). These names might be an attempt to flatter the owner of the vessel, but it is more likely that they refer to God. These names come directly out of descriptions in the Qur'an, which provides ninety-nine names of God, each highlighting an aspect of his divine character.

If we had the complete vessels from which these pieces came it would be possible to see that the inscription would likely be repeated around the outside of the entire rim. In Islam, repeating the name of God is an act of piety,[50] and these ceramics subtly create an infinite circle of dedication to God. Potters completed this exercise of religious meditation during the painting of a pot, but the works themselves may have also served as a small reminder of God's unending presence to those who bought them.

Calligraphy can send a powerful message because of its religious origins but it was eventually adapted into new uses and new languages, such as Persian. Although Persian and Arabic are unrelated languages, they look very similar because Persian began to be written with an Arabic script in the Islamic period (similar to the use of Roman script for English, Italian, and German). This bowl (RH 6074), which uses a complicated and colorful technique of overglaze painting called *minai*, incorporates both an Arabic inscription in blue around

Watercolor of fritware bowl decorated in *minai* technique over opaque white glaze, artist unknown.
Oriental Institute, RH 6074

Three fritware sherd decorated with *minai* technique over an opaque white glaze. *Left to right:* OIM A115030, A115026, A115034

the outer rim and verses of Persian poetry in the register below. In Rayy's ceramics, panels of calligraphy seem to be a typical convention of the late Seljuq period (late twelfth/early thirteenth century), when writing was enthusiastically concentrated on ceramics.

Many Persian inscriptions on the vessels from Rayy are verses from popular poetic works of the time, although the examples in this exhibition are too fragmentary to read fully. As a comparison, Persian verses found on more complete ceramics often recall the longing of romantic or spiritual love. No matter what the original subject of calligraphy in Rayy's ceramics, these objects do not only present words. They intertwine the gracefulness of spoken verse into the colors and composition of a three-dimensional object, creating an indivisible work of art.

Abstract Design: Heavenly Gardens in the Secular World

In the same way that beautiful writing is created out of balance and rhythm, the decoration of Rayy's ceramics also relies on patterns, progression, and a subtle sense of ebb and flow. These principles are often expressed through stylized designs of natural forms and twining arabesques, which might be considered the essence of Islamic decoration because they are so ubiquitous in all forms of Islamic art. In the decoration of Rayy's ceramics, these elements come together to create a picture of a culture that is fascinated with gardens. Elements of nature can be found on many types of pottery at Rayy, both glazed and unglazed, whether in the depiction of a small sprig of leaves within a geometric design or whole panels filled with different kinds of vegetation, trellises, streams, and trees. These images may simply represent the shady pleasures of gardens on earth enjoyed by the wealthy elite, but early in the Islamic period these ideas probably merged with the promise in Islam of a heavenly paradise for believers after the Day of Judgment.[51]

In the hot, dry climate of much of the Middle East, the idea of lush gardens with bubbling streams and fragrant plants was naturally attractive. Perhaps with some significance, the English word "paradise" originates from the ancient Persian word for garden, *para-daiza*, meaning a walled park. Gardens existed in Iran long before the Islamic period and early Persian rulers are known to have enjoyed large groves of trees and hunting parks, as well as smaller, more formally designed garden landscapes.[52] It is with the evocative words of the Qur'an, however, that the garden became a symbol of eternal bliss. Many passages in the Qur'an contemplate variations of this idea:

> But those who believe, and do deeds of righteousness, we shall soon admit to Gardens, with rivers flowing beneath, their eternal home: Therein shall they have Companions pure and holy. We shall admit them to shades, cool and ever deepening. — 4:57

> Here is a parable of the Garden which the righteous are promised: In it are rivers of water incorruptible; Rivers of milk of which the taste never changes; rivers of wine, a joy to those who drink; and rivers of honey pure and clear. In it there are for them all kinds of fruits; and Grace from their Lord.... — 47:15

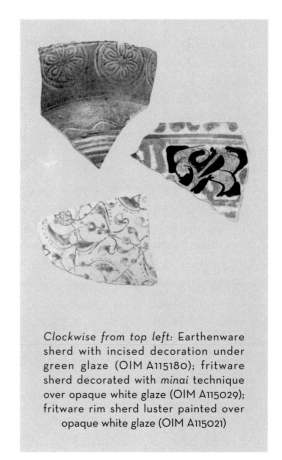

Clockwise from top left: Earthenware sherd with incised decoration under green glaze (OIM A115180); fritware sherd decorated with *minai* technique over opaque white glaze (OIM A115029); fritware rim sherd luster painted over opaque white glaze (OIM A115021)

Cream earthenware sherds with molded decoration. OIM A115147, A115148, A115149

Some of the most extensive gardens among Rayy's ceramics are depicted on the unglazed wares. The heavily decorated curved surfaces of the sherds above (OIM A115147, A115148, A115149) were once part of the rounded walls of jugs or ewers — perfect surfaces for molded and impressed designs. To make these ceramics, clay was pressed into the inside of a mold to form a half-bowl shape. The inside walls of each mold were carved with intricate designs, which the clay would fill and retain as a dimensional surface when it was removed from the mold. Then, two half bowls would be pressed together at the edges to make a round ball-like container; an opening was added at the top and the entire object fired in a kiln. Each of the sherds here has a completely different pattern, which means that they were made using different molds. While the crafting of each mold was a detailed and intensive process, they could be used over and over again to spread the theme of the garden onto many pots.

It is important to note that there is actually no direct connection between the lush vegetation depicted on these ceramics and the heavenly paradise of Islam. They could just as easily depict an appreciation for natural bounties of the earth as the cooling rewards of heaven. Their association with religious meaning is indirect, providing only a hint of the religious backdrop of society, but ready to mesh with its principles. Depending on the perspectives of their users, both Muslims and non-Muslims at Rayy could have found something to appreciate in their beauty.

Fragment of an earthenware ceramic mold. OIM A115125

Figures and Animals: The Many Faces of Rayy

When garden scenes are combined with depictions of people, the context of their meaning is much more clearly secular since figural inspirations in Islamic culture often come from sources beyond religion. One important origin for artistic expression continued to be literature. This charming garden scene is an illustration for one of the most beloved stories of Persian literature, Khusrau and Shirin, which was originally introduced by the twelfth-century poet Nizami in his great romantic epic, the *Khamsa* (Quintet). Although this leaf was painted centuries later, it preserves some of the same decorative techniques that can be seen in the pottery of Rayy. The composition is richly patterned and full of bright colors. Vegetation undulates across the page, creating a rhythm to the story line as the two lovers Khusrau and Shirin meet in the cool shade of tents under a golden sky. The prominence of the figures is the most striking — or perhaps surprising — aspect in this painting since it is often assumed that representations of living creatures is forbidden in Islamic tradition.

Shirin meeting with Khusrau. 1525/1550, Iran. Opaque watercolor and gold on paper, 6 x 4 1/4 in. Collection of the Art Institute of Chicago, Gift of Ann McNear. 1975.510

Cream earthenware sherd with incised decoration (OIM A115040); fritware sherd luster-painted over opaque white glaze (OIM A115018); fritware sherd decorated with *minai* technique over opaque white glaze (OIM A115032); cream earthenware sherd with molded decoration (OIM A115043)

Compared to the cultures around it, Islamic art does have relatively fewer depictions of animals and people. This phenomenon stems from the traditions of Islam, which discourages representations of the human form, maintaining that God should be the only creator. There is no explicit prohibition against figurative art in the Qur'an itself but rather warnings against idolatry. Following these values in the earliest days of Islam, the prophet Muhammad cleared the holy shrine at Mecca in Arabia of idols and other images. In addition, *Hadith* literature, a collection of anecdotes describing the words and deeds of Muhammad, states more clearly that someone who produces or owns pictures will be in a weak position on the Day of Judgment.[53]

Nevertheless, it is a misconception that Islamic cultures actively forbid the uses of human or animal figures in art. In reality, the restriction is mainly based on context. In public areas or religious buildings, for example, intricate and beautiful geometric patterns, arabesques, and calligraphy predominate out of respect for religious values. At Rayy, excavations revealed large mosques and other administrative buildings in the Governmental Quarter, whose walls were decorated with wonderfully patterned stucco-work. No figural designs were found in this setting; however, Rayy's private neighborhoods present a different side of Islamic culture. Figural art is often found in these non-religious contexts, albeit in a restrained manner. Figures were most often seen in the vibrant miniature paintings in the manuscripts of the upper classes, but also in ceramic decoration.

Since few manuscript paintings survive from the period when Rayy was at its height, ceramics provide the most important evidence for the ways that Rayy's people visualized themselves. Like the examples shown above (OIM A115040, A115018, A115032, A115043), the images of faces and figures on ceramics are extremely varied in conception. In many of these sherds the human face has been carefully and cleverly abstracted, becoming pure decoration through a lack of individualized features. These figures tell us little about the realities of physical appearance of people at Rayy but this was a purposeful decision on the part of the craftsmen. Across the Islamic world most ceramic artists drew from a standard repertoire of conventions in figure drawing and rarely depicted specific individuals in portrait. Perhaps even in secular contexts artists were influenced by religion and held back from re-creating reality too closely, leaving that task to God.

Although ceramics do not show a clear picture of the actual people of Rayy, they still have much to say about them. More than other types of decoration, the figural depictions on Rayy's ceramics are clearly influenced by the diversity of cultures that made this city a home. The figures on this late twelfth/early thirteenth century bowl (RE 979) have influences of Turkish culture and a strong feeling of the Silk Roads. Their rounded moon faces are associated with the literary Turkic ideals,[54] reflecting the impact of Central Asian culture on Iran after the Seljuq migrations into Persia in the twelfth century.

Fragment of cream earthenware bowl with molded decoration. Oriental Institute, RE 979

Animals of all types are also depicted on Rayy's ceramics, including familiar animals such as birds, horses, fish, cats, dogs, hedgehogs, bulls, gazelles, as well as more exotic species like leopards and elephants. In some cases, these figures may be a reflection of the environment around Rayy that took the potter's fancy. However, depictions of certain animals were common throughout the Islamic world and over long periods, probably because they were symbols of values or had metaphorical meaning. In the Islamic conception, the zodiac of the night sky was populated by many animals, each associated a with certain fortune. Other animals were portrayed with more complex nuance. The name "gazelle" (which was adapted into English from the Arabic) is closely related to a type of fancifully rhymed poetry that became popular in tenth-century Iran called *ghazal*.

Watercolor of fritware bowl painted in black under transparent turquoise glaze, artist unknown. Oriental Institute, RE 2828

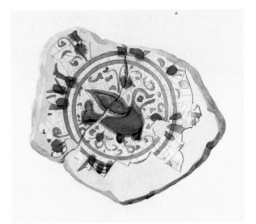

Top row from left: Cream earthenware sherd with incised decoration (OIM A115041); fritware sherd decorated in *minai* technique over opaque white glaze (OIM A115025); fritware sherd decorated in *minai* technique over opaque white glaze (OIM A115008); cream earthenware sherd with molded decoration (OIM A115049)

Bottom row from left: Watercolor of base of earthenware bowl with white slip and incised decoration under transparent glaze, artist unknown (Oriental Institute, RCH 1325); watercolor of fritware sherd, luster and blue decoration over opaque white glaze, artist unknown (Oriental Institute, RD 2353); watercolor of base of a vessel painted in blue and black under transparent glaze, artist unknown (Oriental Institute, RCi 3758, 3759)

INDUSTRY AND INNOVATION

The close connections of the Islamic world took many forms, whether through politics, trade, religious ideology, or migration. These are not just abstract concepts of exchange; they all imply the close involvement of people. The same is true of the shared ceramic traditions in Islamic culture. Rayy's ceramics help to address a number of questions about the people who sponsored a formal ceramic industry: How did people involve themselves with producing, buying, and selling ceramics? Who helped spread ceramic technology and how important was this exchange?

In the modern world, few people would consider ceramic making to be a ground-breaking technology. Since ceramics were used so widely in the medieval Middle East, however, new developments of ceramic design and color could be considered fashionable items of popular culture. Innovations must have impressed potential buyers and spurred even further production, making the ceramic industry an important forum for creative experimentation.

Issues surrounding the ceramic industry may be best addressed by focusing on one period in greater depth. The best opportunity for this at Rayy is the Seljuq period (mid-eleventh to the mid-thirteenth century), which is represented by a large number of ceramic finds from Schmidt's excavations. The Seljuq period also witnessed momentous changes in ceramic technology which have long attracted scholars and have been the focus of intense research. In addition, the workings of the ceramic industry during this time are still not well understood, so archaeological studies are extremely relevant for future research.

One of the most remarkable characteristics of Seljuq period ceramics is how quickly new innovations traveled from place to place over wide areas, from North Africa to Central Asia. Trade was probably a factor, but societies often thrive on the movement of ideas as much as the movement of objects. Islamic ceramics in particular are the outcome of a dynamic exchange involving a large community of craftsmen and artists who traveled widely and passed their technical knowledge on to apprentices and colleagues. The individuality of local markets was always important, and it can be fairly easy to distinguish between the ceramics of different regions, and at times even the ceramics of different cities. However, it is hard to dispute the notion that the ceramic industry as a whole operated in a wider regional context.

It not possible to discuss the whole story of the Seljuq ceramic industry through Rayy since it was only one place in a large network of common exchange. However, as a cultural hub Rayy's ceramics were influenced by the spread of cultural ideas and the city provides a good reference point within the exchange system. The connections between cities involved in the network of trade are most apparent in glazed or highly decorated ceramics, many of which can be considered valued luxury wares. Glazed luxury ceramics make up a small percentage of all the artifacts found in the Rayy excavations — the most common ceramics are unglazed — but they provide a good measure for technological development during the Seljuq period.

Ceramic Industry at Rayy

Simple unglazed pots could have been made in any of Rayy's households using a few simple tools and a small kiln, but the sheer number of ceramics found at Rayy indicates that pottery making was a very profitable industry in the medieval period. Most of Rayy's ceramics were probably made in professional workshops which flooded the market with a variety of standardized forms.

Manuscript detail. Collection of the Art Institute of Chicago, Gift of Ann McNear. 1980.334

A man's death outside a pottery shop. 1570/1580, Iran, Shiraz. Opaque watercolor on paper, 7 5/8 x 4 in. Collection of the Art Institute of Chicago, Gift of Ann McNear. 1980.334

Watercolor of fritware spouted jar with turquoise glaze, artist unknown (Oriental Institute, RH 6147); watercolor of fritware jug painted in luster over opaque white glaze, artist unknown (Oriental Institute, RH 4463); watercolor of fritware bowl with transparent glaze and blue-and-purple splashed decoration, artist unknown (Oriental Institute, RE 3463)

Rayy's potters were not only artists; they were also businessmen. This picture of a ceramic shop (1980.334) comes down to us almost by accident since it is the setting that took an illustrator's fancy within a more serious narrative of prose on Sufism, a mystical sect of Islam. The man lying on the ground in front of the pottery shop has likely given up his life so that he may return to God. The basic layout of ceramic shops in Rayy was probably quite similar to the one depicted in this illustration, although the latter was created centuries after the cultural acme of Rayy. Potters were not limited to selling a single type of pottery or even objects of one type of glaze. Bowls, vases, jugs, and ewers would all have been laid out for display, a rainbow to delight the eyes of a customer.

Ceramics were traditionally sold in most Islamic cities in central markets which concentrated the exchange of goods in urban areas. During the Islamic period Rayy was widely known as an important commercial center and historical sources relate that up to eight large bazaars were dispersed throughout the city.[55] Ceramics would presumably have been sold in many of these areas to meet the needs of the surrounding neighborhoods.

The management of ceramic workshops often passed down through generations of a family, and this was probably a respected career since contemporary historical sources mention ceramic makers with high regard. Many potters were also highly literate, evidenced by ceramics with calligraphic inscriptions from the Qur'an and other literary sources. Even with these sophisticated designs and high-end products, it seems that the majority of potters were dependent upon a large commercial market since there is little evidence for royal or court patronage of ceramics at Rayy or in other cities.

Potters must have moved frequently throughout the streets of Rayy between their kilns, workshops, and street-front shops. Ceramic kilns produce ill-smelling smoke and for this reason they were often located at the edges of Islamic period towns and cities.[56] The one kiln found in the excavations at Rayy conforms to this arrangement since it was situated at the northern outskirts of the central city on the Cheshmeh Ali mound.[57] If kilns were also built within Rayy's walls, potters would have needed to be very careful with the continuously burning fires needed for ceramic production. The closely intertwined buildings in market areas were not appropriate for safely conducting these activities, so Rayy's potters must have carried many of their wares from demarcated kiln areas into city shops for sale.

Technology and Creativity

In Seljuq period Persia innovations in the ceramic industry occurred both in the makeup of the ceramic body with the invention of fritware and in the use of increasingly elaborate glaze techniques. Together, these elements offered ceramic artists a whole new range of decorative possibilities. For this reason the Seljuq period is often called the golden age of Islamic art.

The finely shaped bowls below capture a sense of the wide range of creativity and skill of Rayy's potters in various qualities and styles. All are similar in shape, with a high base and very thin flaring walls, a popular style in Persian ceramic workshops of the late twelfth/early thirteenth century. The delicate quality of these forms was made possible by the use of fritware, a compound of ground quartz and clay that was meant to mimic the white clarity of Chinese porcelain. Fritware has great strength and could be formed into a variety of shapes not easily accomplished with other, less malleable clays of the Middle East.

The basic origin of fritware technology and its spread across the Islamic world is still not fully understood. Several scholars have proposed an origin in the workshops of Fatimid Egypt sometime in the mid- to late eleventh century, but others have proposed a separate Persian development.[58] The most likely scenario, however, is that Egyptian potters themselves traveled into Syria and Iran, bringing knowledge of fritware technology with them, since this type of ware seems to appear suddenly at Persian sites in the late twelfth century.[59] There are no surviving historical records that confirm these journeys, but it is difficult to imagine that ceramic technology spread without the active involvement of ceramic makers.

The transition from using earthenwares to using fritwares at Rayy did not happen overnight. Fritware was gradually adapted into the established ceramic traditions, and the new technology inspired new creativity. Many fritwares were excavated alongside earthenware ceramics, indicating that the two techniques were used concurrently, but fritwares quickly became the preferred medium for decorative experimentation. The potters who made the bowls shown below (OIM A115084/RB 979; OIM A115185, A115186/RE 2835; OIM A115143/RG 4020) took advantage of glazing techniques that complement the properties of fritware, marking an important change from the styles

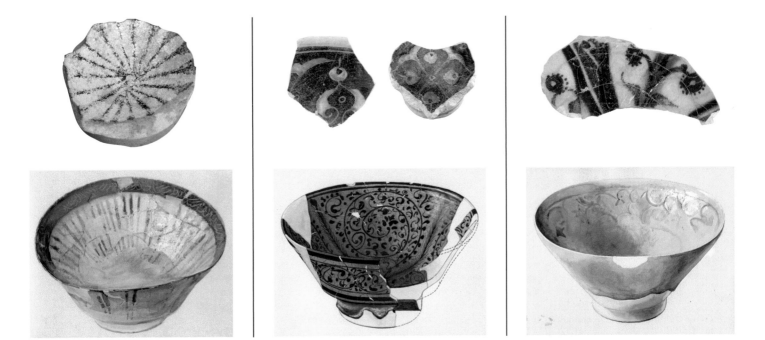

Left: Base of fritware vessel painted in blue under transparent glaze (OIM A115084); watercolor of fritware bowl painted in blue and black under transparent glaze, artist unknown (Oriental Institute, RB 979)

Center: Fragments of fritware bowl with black slip and carved decoration under transparent turquoise glaze (OIM A115185, A115186); watercolor of fritware bowl painted in black under turquoise glaze, artist unknown (Oriental Institute, RE 2835)

Right: Base of vessel, fritware painted in blue and black under transparent glaze (OIM A115143); watercolor of fritware bowl with incised decoration under transparent turquoise glaze, artist unknown (Oriental Institute, RG 4020)

of earlier ceramics. Potters found the white color of fritware desirable in itself without slips or opaque glazes. Only transparent glazes were applied, which simplified the production process and allowed artists to paint boldly colored designs onto the ceramic beneath the glaze. Floriated panels, radiating stripes, and the fine strokes of calligraphy are common in this period, both at Rayy and in the larger regions of Iran and Syria. The combination of fritware and underglazing techniques would become the dominant method for crafting fine Islamic ceramics through to the modern period. This technique even spread to Islamic Spain and was adopted in Europe, where it served as the inspiration for European majolica ceramics.

Ceramic-making techniques were generally passed down orally and taught by example and therefore few descriptions of the fritware recipe exist. One source which does survive comes from a historian of the Mongol court, Abu al-Qasim 'Abdallah bin 'Ali bin Muhammad al-Qashani. His alchemical treatise, "The Virtues of Jewels and the Delicacies of Fragrances," written in the year 1300, contains an epilogue on the art of ceramics. In it he discusses the raw materials needed for the making of fritwares, the qualities of different glazes, and formulas for luster-painted ceramics. Although it is unknown whether Abu al-Qasim himself practiced this craft, he came from a leading family of potters from Kashan, so his information is probably first hand. His recipe for fritware is detailed, and only a small excerpt of the process is given here:

> ...if they want to compound a body out of which to make pottery objects and vessels such as dishes, basins, jugs and house tiles, they take ten parts of the afore-mentioned white *shukar-i sang* [quartz], ground and sieved through coarse silk, and one part of ground glass frit mixed together and one part of white Luri clay dissolved in water. This is kneaded well like dough and left to mature for one night. In the morning it is well beaten by hand and the mastercraftsman makes it into fine vessels on the potter's wheel; these are left standing till they are half dry. They are scraped down on the wheel and the feet are added, and when they are dry they are washed with a damp linen cloth in order to smooth over the lines on them so that they disappear. When they are dry again they are rubbed with a wool cloth until they are clean and smooth. — Allen, "Abu'l-Qasim's Treatise on Ceramics," pp. 113–14

THE LUSTERWARE RECIPES OF ABU AL-QASIM

Lusterwares were one of the most technologically advanced ceramics of the Seljuq period and different pottery workshops developed their own variations on the best recipes. These specialties are visible in the different consistencies and colors of luster glaze in different regions and time periods. The historian Abu al-Qasim 'Abdallah bin 'Ali bin Muhammad al-Qashani provides a technical discussion on one formula for twice-fired lusterware in his alchemical treatise "The Virtues of Jewels and the Delicacies of Fragrances":

> Those that come out of the firing white they paint with the enamel of two firings.... The enamel is composed as follows: take one and a half *mans* of red and yellow arsenic, one *man* of gold and silver marcasite, one *batman* of Tisi yellow vitriol and a quarter of roasted copper, and mix it to a paste and grind it. A quarter of this is mixed with six *dirhams* of pure silver which has been burned and ground and is ground on a stone for twenty-four hours until it is extremely fine. Dissolve this in some grape juice or vinegar and paint it onto the vessels as desired, and place them in a second kiln specially made for this purpose, and give them light smoke for 72 hours until they acquire the colour of two firings. When they are cold take them out and rub them with damp earth so that the colour of gold comes out.... That which has been evenly fired reflects like red gold and shines like the light of the sun.
>
> — Allen, "Abu'l-Qasim's Treatise on Ceramics," p. 114

Movements of Pots, Movements of People

At the same time that fritware was spreading throughout the Middle East, another form of ceramic technology — lusterware — was enjoying rejuvenation. Rayy's specific role in the manufacture of luxury ceramics such as lusterwares has long been a contested subject. The debate typically centers on whether these ceramics were produced at Rayy or imported from other nearby centers known for their high-quality products, for example, the city of Kashan, about 150 miles south of Rayy. Unfortunately, excavations at Rayy do not provide direct access into ceramic manufacture during the Seljuq period. At least one kiln was found in the excavations,[60] but it is unclear in what periods it was used. In addition, no pottery shops from the Seljuq period were identified, probably because excavations were not conducted in market areas. However, the products of the ceramic industry at Rayy — the pots that people bought and used — are still accessible and can help guide scholars toward a better understanding of ceramic manufacture at Rayy.

Earthenware sherds luster painted over opaque white glaze. *Clockwise from top left:* OIM A115140, A115139, A115141, A115142

Rayy is now doubted as a major production center for lusterwares and other fine ceramics because of the political troubles the city experienced in the late twelfth century. As a result of clashes between different religious sects in 1186 and after, about half of the population is said to have fled the city, greatly reducing the market for luxury ceramics. Nevertheless, the Rayy excavations revealed many luxury ceramics from this period and it is therefore likely that production of some luxury wares continued and the ceramic industry functioned successfully at Rayy. The end results of the ceramic industry at Rayy — the pots that people bought and used — are useful evidence for confirming the impact of lusterware at Rayy. These show that Rayy's ceramics, including lusterwares, were a part of an important local industry.

By the start of the Seljuq period, the technique of luster painting had already been known for centuries in the Islamic world — and also at Rayy (OIM A115140, A115139, A115141, A115142). Luster may have first been used in the eighth century in Egypt and Syria to decorate glass;[61] by the ninth century it was being used to deco-rate ceramics in Abbasid Persia. Lusterwares and opaque whitewares of the same period both employed a creamy white background glaze. Lusterwares, however, required the additional technical skills of glaze mixing and firing. Each luster vessel had to be fired twice, once for the white glaze base and a second time after the application of a metallic solution consisting of metal compounds of silver and copper oxide.

Small dish. The David Collection, Copenhagen. 14/1988

Luster ceramics had wide appeal and were distributed and imitated throughout the Islamic world. Lusterwares from this early period have been found at Rayy, but these examples are very limited and are so similar to the lusterwares produced in Iraq that they are likely to be products of trade. After the mid-tenth century, lusterwares appear to have lost their appeal both in Rayy and in other areas of the Abbasid empire, but luster decoration never died out in the Islamic world. It continued to thrive in Fatimid Egypt and in the twelfth century again appeared throughout Syria and Persia.

This sherd from a lusterware jug (OIM A115014/RH 4759) from the Rayy excavations is an important artifact that connects the city directly to the wider popularity of lusterwares in the twelfth century. The sherd comes from the Syrian tradition of luster ceramics, which were themselves stylistically based on Egyptian lusterwares. The large band of text around the body of the jug reads *baraka* "blessing." The rich brown of the luster, the angular style of the kufic writing, and the leaflets coiled into the letters can all be found in similar Syrian lusterwares.

It is difficult to determine whether the luster artifacts from the Rayy excavations were actually made at Rayy, but the existence of objects such as the lusterware jug raises new questions about the relationships between ceramic makers and consumers in Iran, Syria, and Egypt in the Seljuq period. Rayy's ceramic industry may have been much more closely related to that of Syria than is typically thought, which, if true, confirms the potential of the people of different regions in the Islamic world to influence each other. It is likely that Syrian potters had begun to move into Iran — even to Rayy — bringing some of their wares with them since as the popularity of lusterware continued to grow it developed a more uniquely Iranian style.

The spread of lusterware production in general is not likely

Rim of vessel, fritware luster painted over opaque white glaze (OIM A115014); watercolor reconstruction of the jug, artist unknown (Oriental Institute, RH 4759)

to have occurred through experimentation at unrelated workshops since the precise mixture of ingredients and high technicality needed for its production were very difficult to achieve. Many scholars consider it more likely that potters played a direct role in spreading luster techniques through their own movements from place to place. There is temptation to link the movements of potters with social and political disturbances, for example, the appearance of luster workshops in Syria and Persia soon after political turmoil in Egypt as a result of the Crusades and the termination of the Fatimid dynasty.[62] However appealing the connections between material culture and political events may be, they can be very difficult to prove, and it is first necessary to focus on individual centers of ceramic production instead. Even this can be difficult since few Iranian archaeological sites have been scientifically excavated to a significant extent, but Rayy at least offers one of the few examples of securely contextualized lusterware, confirmed to be used and discarded at the site.

The excavations within the walled city at Rayy have revealed small concentrations of luster sherds that display a great variety of decoration. Most of Rayy's lusterware ceramics do not show direct connections to Syrian workshops but rather are a Persian interpretation of earlier or even contiguous themes of Egyptian and Syrian luster. The lusterware designs consist primarily of either a "monumental" style, where figures are painted in reserve against a luster background, or a "miniature" style, where the luster stands out against a white background.[63] The decorative themes are diverse, from calligraphic panels to abstracted shapes such as crosses and to detailed figural compositions. The range of luster ceramics at Rayy suggests more than sporadic trade connections with other Persian ceramic centers such as Kashan. If these ceramics were in demand by Rayy's residents, it would have been much more profitable for a prestigious ceramic workshop in another city to have a shop in Rayy itself, or to collaborate with local potters.

Fritware rim sherd from a jug; luster painted over turquoise glaze in opaque white glaze (OIM A115199); watercolor reconstruction of the jug, artist unknown (Oriental Institute, RH 6433)

Fritware bowl sherd luster painted over opaque white glaze (OIM A115132); watercolor reconstruction of the bowl, artist unknown (Oriental Institute, RH 6118)

  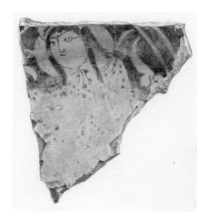

Luster paint over opaque white glaze. *Left to right:* OIM A115017, A115192; watercolor by unknown artist. Oriental Institute, RE 3127

CONCLUSION: RAYY TODAY

DONALD WHITCOMB

When Schmidt left the site of Rayy and departed Tehran for the last time in 1937, he no doubt hoped to return to finish the work. He doubtless also hoped to bring his results to publication. But the years passed and neither hope was fulfilled. Even while he worked at Rayy, land prices were rising and permissions to dig from land owners were increasingly difficult to obtain. Behind the hill upon which the citadel was built was already a cement factory, a modern industry which has now eaten into the mountain and severely damaged the area; the backdrop of the antiquities is now the highways and skyscrapers of modern Tehran. Within the inner city of Rayy, the mosque and *madrasas* are partially infringed upon by a large glycerin factory. Isolate villages and even the town of Bibi Zubaidah and the shrine of Shah 'Abd al-Azim are now engulfed in the houses and streets of the southern suburbs of modern Tehran.

The archaeological site has not been completely forgotten. There have been Iranian archaeological projects, such as those led by Chahriyar Adle, and scholarly studies, such as the volumes of Hussein Karimian. Most recently, Dr. Hassan Fazeli, Director of the Iranian Research Center for Archaeology, has conducted new research for over a decade in the remnants of the mound that has been transformed into a small neighborhood park. The process of development, which had begun in the days of Schmidt, continues to destroy the vestiges of antiquity. This is a pattern of progress found all over the world and usually so subtle and seductive that the past is obliterated before the loss is realized.

Gathering for traditional washing of new carpets at the spring in Rayy.
Photo taken in 1970s by Donald Whitcomb

The excavations of Erich Schmidt take on a special meaning for those who would remember the wonders of Rayy and accomplishment of medieval Persia. It is hard to imagine old notes and sherds of pottery as embodiments of a civilization, but these results of archaeological research from long ago provide just that — pieces for the imagination to relive the many stories of the past. We may now enjoy this experience in Chicago and we hope that someday the people of modern Rayy will share in this inheritance.

Medieval Rayy is only one of the archaeological settlements now devoured by Tehran. Schmidt also excavated the ancient site of Cheshmeh Ali, a small prehistoric settlement at the foot of the natural spring of the same name. In the course of the millennia this water source inspired settlement after settlement and ultimately the famous medieval metropolis of Rayy. Tehran, the modern-day metropolitan capital of Iran, still values the spring for ceremonial washing of newly made Persian carpets. The presence of this bountiful freshwater spring in a naturally parched and arid region was responsible for the continuity of life for some 8,000 years.

ENDNOTES

Ray: From Wallis to Watson

[1] Wallis, *The Godman Collection*, pl. 29, figs. 7–8.

[2] Pope, "*Survey of Persian Art* and Its Critics," p. 186.

[3] Sarre, "Fruhislamische, in Graffiatotechnik dekorierte Keramik persischer Herkunft," p. 46.

[4] Ettinghausen, "Evidence for the Identification of Kashan Pottery."

[5] See, for example, Lane, *Early Islamic Pottery*.

[6] Watson, "Persian Lustre-Painted Pottery: The Rayy and Kashan Styles."

Introduction to the Exhibition

[7] For a short summary of the different archaeological periods of settlement found at Rayy, see Schmidt, *Flights over Ancient Cities of Iran*, p. 29.

[8] al-Muqaddasi, *Best Divisions for Knowledge*, p. 347.

Erich Schmidt's Excavations at Rayy

[9] For the original accounts, see the following publications: Morier, *Journey through Persia*, pp. 232 and 403; Porter, *Travels in Georgia*, vol. 1, pp. 357–64; and Ousely, *Travels in Various Countries of the East*, vol. 3, pp. 174–99.

[10] Schmidt, "Rayy Excavation Report I."

[11] Schmidt, *Flights over Ancient Cities of Iran*, p. 29.

[12] Schmidt, "Rayy Spring Season 1936."

[13] Vernoit, "The Rise of Islamic Archaeology," p. 8.

[14] Schmidt, "Rayy Expedition Report II."

[15] Schmidt, "Rayy Excavations – Season 1935."

[16] Schmidt, "Rayy Spring Season 1936."

[17] The specific challenge of presenting archaeological material in museums has been well addressed by a number of authors in the field of Museum Studies. See Clarke, "Poor Museums, Rich Men's Media"; and Pearce, "Museum Studies in Material Culture."

Selections from the Exhibition

[18] For a concise discussion on the definition of Islamic art, see Folsach, *Islamic Art*, pp. 16–21.

[19] Perry, "Isfidhabaj, Blancmanger and No Almonds," p. 265.

[20] Arberry, "A Baghdad Cookery Book."

[21] Perry, "Elements of Arab Feasting," p. 230.

[22] Wilkinson, *Nishapur*, p. xlii.

[23] al-Muqaddasi, *Best Divisions for Knowledge*, p. 348.

[24] Grube, *Islamic Pottery in the Keir Collection*, pp. 244–45.

[25] Watson, *Ceramics from Islamic Lands*, p. 325.

[26] Ettinghausen, "Uses of Sphero-Conical Vessels," p. 222.

[27] Hildburgh, "Aeolipiles as Fire-Blowers."

[28] Ghouchani and Adle, "A Sphero-Conical Vessel as Fuqqā'a."

[29] Keall, "One Man's Mede Is another Man's Persian."

[30] Ghouchani and Adle, "A Sphero-Conical Vessel as Fuqqā'a."

[31] Pentz, "A Medieval Workshop," pp. 89-93. For an illustration of the "grenade," see Riis and Poulsen, *Les verreries et poteries medievales.*

[32] Bulliet, "Conversion to Islam."

[33] Bosworth et al., eds., *Encyclopaedia of Islam.*

[34] These types of ceramics have been labeled as a "yellow-ware" family. See Watson, "Report on the Glazed Ceramics."

[35] There are many archaeological sites that provide evidence of the importance of Gulf Coast trade in many periods. For specific examples, see Tampoe, *Maritime Trade between China and the West;* Kennet, *Sasanian and Islamic Pottery;* and Kervran, Hiebert, and Rougeulle, *Qal'at Al-Bahrain.*

[36] Williamson, "Regional Distribution of Mediaeval Persian Pottery," p. 16.

[37] Tonghini, *Qal'at Ja'bar Pottery.*

[38] Finster, "The Saljuqs as Patrons," p. 22; and Whitehouse, "Maritime Trade in the Gulf."

[39] Tabbaa, "Bronze Shapes in Iranian Ceramics," p. 110.

[40] Watson, *Ceramics from Islamic Lands,* p. 55.

[41] al-Hamawi, *Dictionnaire géographique,* p. 274.

[42] Bosworth et al., eds., *Encyclopaedia of Islam,* p. 472.

[43] Misfired and malformed sherds have been found at Rayy from this period. These are wasters from ceramic production and would not have been transported, so they provide fairly secure evidence for the ceramic industry at Rayy.

[44] De Clavijo, *Embassy to Tamerlane,* p. 167.

[45] Watson, *Ceramics from Islamic Lands,* p. 238.

[46] Gray, *Studies in Chinese and Islamic Art,* p. 95.

[47] See Piotrovsky, *On Islamic Art,* p. 36.

[48] Khatibi and Sijelmassi, *The Splendour of Islamic Calligraphy.*

[49] The relationships between early calligraphic variations are discussed by Déroche, *The Abbasid Tradition.*

[50] Piotrovsky, *On Islamic Art,* p. 35.

[51] Blair and Bloom, *Images of Paradise in Islamic Art,* pp. 15–17.

[52] Von Folsach, Lunbaek, and Mortensen, eds., *Sultan, Shah, and Great Mughal,* p. 229.

[53] Von Folsach, *Islamic Art,* p. 17.

[54] Pancaroğlu, *Perpetual Glory,* p. 127.

[55] *Encyclopedia of Islam,* s.v. "Al-Istakhri," p. 471. See also "Al-Istakhri" in Ouseley, trans., *Oriental Geography of Ebn Haukal,* pp. 176–77.

[56] Wilkinson, *Nishapur,* p. xxxiii.

[57] Schmidt, "Rayy Excavation Report I – May 1934."

[58] Grube, *Cobalt and Lustre,* pp. 148–49.

[59] Watson, *Ceramics from Islamic Lands,* p. 41.

[60] This kiln was found in excavations on the Cheshmeh Ali mound along with great numbers of slags and pottery wasters.

[61] Fehérvári, *Ceramics of the Islamic Lands in the Tareq Rajab Museum,* p. 42.

[62] A concise review of these arguments is provided by Watson, *Persian Lustre Ware,* p. 26.

[63] Monumental and miniature styles of lusterware were explored in depth by Oliver Watson and are now used to differentiate lusterware types in most major publications.

SELECTED BIBLIOGRAPHY

Adle, C., and Y. Kossari. "Notes sur les première et seconde campagnes archéologiques à Rey." In *Contribution à l'histoire de l'Iran: Mélanges offerts à Jean Perrot*, edited by F. Vallat, pp. 295–307. Paris: Éditions Recherche sur les Civilisations, 1990.

Allen, James. "Abū'l-Qāsim's Treatise on Ceramics." *Iran* 11 (1973): 111–20.

al-Hamawi, Yaqut ibn ʿAbd Allah. *Dictionnaire géographique, historique et littéraire de la Perse et des contrées adjacentes, extrait du Modjem el-bouldan de Yaqout, et complété à l'aide de documents arabes et persans*, edited by C. Barbier de Meynard. Paris: l'Imprimerie impériale, 1861.

al-Muqaddasi. *The Best Divisions for Knowledge of the Regions: A Translation of Aḥsan Al-Taqāsīm Fī Maʿrifat Al-Aqālīm*, translated by Basil Anthony Collins. The Great Books of Islamic Civilization. Reading, UK: Garnet Publishing, 1995.

Arberry, A. J. "A Baghdad Cookery Book (Kitab Al-Tabikh)." In *Medieval Arab Cookery*, by Maxine Rodinson, A. J. Arberry, and Charles Perry, pp. 19–89. Devon: Prospect Books, 2001.

Bates, Daniel G., and Fred Plog. *Cultural Anthropology*. New York: McGraw Hill, 1990.

Blair, Sheila S., and Jonathan M. Bloom. *Images of Paradise in Islamic Art*. Hanover, NH: Hood Museum of Art, Dartmouth College, 1991.

Bosworth, C. E.; E. Van Donzel; W. P. Heinrichs; and G. Lecomte, eds. *Encyclopaedia of Islam*. Leiden: E. J. Brill.

Bulliet, Richard W. "Conversion to Islam and the Emergence of a Muslim Society in Iran." In *Conversion to Islam: A Comparative Study of Islamization*, edited by N. Levtzion, pp. 30–51. New York: Holmes & Meier, 1979.

Clarke, D. V. "Poor Museums, Rich Men's Media: An Archaeological Perspective." In *Extracting Meaning from the Past*, edited by John Bintliff, pp. 44–49. Oxford: Oxbow Books, 1988.

González de Clavijo, Ruy. *Embassy to Tamerlane, 1403–1406*, translated by Guy Le Strange. London: Routledge, 1928.

Déroche, François. *The Abbasid Tradition: Qurans of the 8th to the 10th Centuries*. New York: Nour Foundation in association with Azimuth Editions and Oxford University Press, 1992.

Ettinghausen, Richard. "Evidence for the Identification of Kashan Pottery," *Ars Islamica* 3 (1936): 44–75.

——. "The Uses of Sphero-Conical Vessels in the Muslim East." *Journal of Near Eastern Studies* 24 (1965): 218–29.

Fehérvári, Géza. *Ceramics of the Islamic Lands in the Tareq Rajab Museum*. London: I. B. Tauris, 2000.

Finster, Barbara. "The Saljuqs as Patrons." In *The Art of the Saljuqs in Iran and Anatolia: Proceedings of a Symposium Held in Edinburgh in 1982*, edited by Robert Hillenbrand, pp. 17–28. Islamic Art and Architecture 4. Costa Mesa, CA: Mazda Publishers, 1994.

Folsach, Kjeld von. *Islamic Art: The David Collection*. Copenhagen: Davids Samling, 1990.

Folsach, Kyeld von; Torben Lunbaek; and Peder Mortensen. *Sultan, Shah, and Great Mughal: The History and Culture of the Islamic World*. Copenhagen: National Museum, 1996.

Ghouchani, A., and Chahyar Adle. "A Sphero-Conical Vessel as Fuqqāʿa, or a Gourd for 'Beer.'" *Muqarnas* 9 (1992): 72–92.

Gray, Basil. *Studies in Chinese and Islamic Art*. Two volumes. London: Pindar Press, 1985–1987.

Grube, Ernst J. *Cobalt and Lustre: The First Centuries of Islamic Pottery*. Nasser D. Makhalili Collection of Islamic Art 9. London: Nour Foundation in association with Azimuth Editions and Oxford University Press, 1995.

——. *Islamic Pottery of the Eighth to the Fifteenth Century in the Keir Collection*. London: Faber & Faber Limited, 1976.

Hildburgh, W. L. "Aeolipiles as Fire-Blowers." *Archaeologia* 94 (1951): 27–55.

Holy Quran, with English translation by Mohammad Marmaduke Pickthall and Urdu translation by Fateh Mohammed Jallendhri. Delhi: Kutub Khana Ishaat-ul-Islam, 1970.

Karīmān, Ḥusayn. *Qaṣran (Kūhsarān) imabāḥis-i tarīkhī va jughrāfīya'ī va ijtimā'ī va maz'habī va vaṣf-i ātishgāh, minṭaqah-i kūhistānī-Rayy-i bāstān va Tihrān-i Knūnī*. Two volumes. Tehran: Anjuman-i Āsār-i Millī, 1977.

Keall, Edward J. "One Man's Mede Is Another Man's Persian; One Man's Coconut Is Another Man's Grenade." In "Essays in Honor of Oleg Grabar," special issue, *Muqarnas* 10 (1993): 275-85.

———. "The Topography and Architecture of Medieval Rayy." *Akten des 7. Internationalen Kongresses für Iranische Kunst und Archäologie: München, 7.–10. September 1976*. Archäologische Mitteilungen aus Iran, Ergänzungsband 6, pp. 537-44. Berlin: Dietrich Reimer, 1979.

Keall, E. J., and M. J. Keall. "The Qal'eh-i Yazdigird Pottery: A Statistical Approach." *Iran* 19 (1981): 33-80.

Kennet, Derek. *Sasanian and Islamic Pottery from Ras Al-Khaimah: Classification, Chronology and Analysis of Trade in the Western Indian Ocean*. Bar International Series 1248. Oxford: Archaeopress, 2004.

Kervran, Monique; Fredrik Hiebert; and Axelle Rougeulle. *Qal'at Al-Bahrain: A Trading and Military Outpost 3rd Millennium B.C. – 17th Century A.D.* Turnhout: Brepols, 2005.

Khatibi, Abdelkebir, and Mohammed Sijelmassi. *The Splendour of Islamic Calligraphy*. London: Thames & Hudson, 1994.

Kleiss, W. "Čal Tarkhan südöstlich von Rey." *Archäologische Mitteilungen aus Iran* 20 (1987): 309-18.

———. "Qal'eh Gabri, Naqarah Khaneh und Bordj-e Yazid bei Reyy." *Archäologische Mitteilungen aus Iran* 15 (1982): 311-28.

Kroeber, A. L., and Clyde Kluckhohn. *Culture: A Critical Review of Concepts and Definitions*. Papers of the Peabody Museum of American Archaeology and Ethnology, Harvard University 47. Cambridge, MA: The Museum, 1952.

Lane, Arthur. *Early Islamic Pottery: Mesopotamia, Egypt and Persia*. London: Faber & Faber, 1947.

Mason, Robert B. *Shine like the Sun: Lustre-Painted and Associated Pottery from the Medieval Middle East*. Costa Mesa, CA: Mazda, 2004.

Miles, G. C. *The Numismatic History of Rayy*. Numismatic Studies 2. New York: American Numismatic Society, 1938.

———. "A Portrait of the Buyid Prince Rukn al-Dawla." *American Numismatic Society Museum Notes* 11 (1964): 283-93.

Minorsky, V. "Raiy." *Encyclopedia of Islam*. First edition, vol. 3, pp. 1105-08. Leiden: E. J. Brill; London: Luzac, 1913-38.

Minorsky, V., and C. E. Bosworth. "al-Rayy." *Encyclopedia of Islam*. Second edition, vol. 8, pp. 471-73. Leiden: E. J. Brill, 1960-2005.

Morier, James. *A Journey through Persia, Armenia, and Asia Minor, to Constantinople, in the Years 1808 and 1809, in which is Included some Account of the Proceedings of His Majesty's Mission, under Sir Hartford Jones, Bart. K. C. to the Court of the King of Persia*. Philadelphia: M. Carey, 1816.

Ousely, William. *Travels in Various Countries of the East; More Particularly Persia*. London: Rodwell & Martin, 1819-1823.

Ousely, William, translator. *The Oriental Geography of Ebn Haukal, An Arabian Traveller of the Tenth Century*. London: Printed by Wilson for T. Cadell & W. Davies, 1800.

Pancaroğlu, Oya. *Perpetual Glory: Medieval Islamic Ceramics from the Harvey B. Plotnick Collection*. New Haven: Yale University Press, 2007.

Pearce, Susan M. "Museum Studies in Material Culture: Introduction." In *Museum Studies in Material Culture*, edited by Susan M. Pearce, pp. 1-10. London: Leicester University Press, 1989.

Pearce, Susan M., ed. *Museum Studies in Material Culture*. London: Leicester University Press, 1989.

Pentz, Peter. "A Medieval Workshop for Producing 'Greek Fire' Grenades." *Antiquity* 62 (1988): 89–93.

Perry, Charles. "Elements of Arab Feasting." In *Medieval Arab Cookery*, pp. 225–31. Devon: Prospect Books, 2001.

——. "Isfidhabaj, Blancmanger and No Almonds." In *Medieval Arab Cookery*, by Maxime Rodinson and A. J. Arberry, pp. 261–66: Prospect Books, 2001.

Pézard, G., and G. Bondoux. *Mission de Téhéran: II, Reconnaissance du site de Rhages*. Mémoires de la Délégation en Perse 12. Paris: E. Leroux, 1911.

Piotrovsky, Mikhail. *On Islamic Art*. St. Petersburg: State Hermitage Museum, 2001.

Pope, Arthur Upham. "*The Survey of Persian Art* and Its Critics." *Ars Islamica* 9 (1944): 170–208.

Porter, Robert Ker. *Travels in Georgia, Persia, Armenia, Ancient Babylonia, &c. &c. During the Years 1817, 1818, 1819, and 1820*. London: Longman, Hurst, Rees, Orme, & Brown, 1821–22.

Riis, P. J.; V. Poulsen; and Erling Hammershaimb. *Les verreries et poteries médiévales*. Hama: Fouilles et Recherches de la Fondation Carlsberg 1931–1938, Volume 4, Part 2. Copenhagen: National Museum, 1957.

Sarre, Friedrich. "Fruhislamische, in Graffiatotechnik dekorierte Keramik persischer Herkunft in der Islamischen unstabteilun," *Berliner Museen* 35 (1913).

Schmidt, Erich. *Bulletin of the University of Pennsylvania Museum* 5–6. Philadelphia: The Museum, 1935–1936.

——. "Excavations at Rayy." *Ars Islamica* 2 (1935): 139–41.

——. *Flights over Ancient Cities of Iran*. Chicago: University of Chicago Press, 1940.

——. "Rayy Excavation Report I – May 1934." Manuscript housed in the Archives of the Oriental Institute.

——. "Rayy Excavations – Season 1935." Manuscript housed in the Archives of the Oriental Institute.

——. "Rayy Expedition Report II – August 1934." Manuscript housed in the Archives of the Oriental Institute.

——. "Rayy Spring Season 1936." Manuscript housed in the Archives of the Oriental Institute.

Tabbaa, Yasser. "Bronze Shapes in Iranian Ceramics of the Twelfth and Thirteenth Centuries." *Muqarnas* 4 (1987): 98–113.

Tampoe, Moira. *Maritime Trade between China and the West: An Archaeological Study of the Ceramics from Siraf (Persian Gulf), 8th–15th Century A.D.* Bar International Series 555. Oxford: Oxford University Press, 1989.

Tonghini, Christina, and H. H. Franken. *Qal'at Ja'bar Pottery: A Study of a Syrian Fortified Site of the Late 11th–14th Centuries*. Oxford: Oxford University Press, 1998.

Vernoit, Stephen. "The Rise of Islamic Archaeology." *Muqarnas* 14 (1997): 1–10.

Wallis, Henry, *The Godman Collection: Persian Ceramic Art in the Collection of Mr F. Ducane Godman FRS: I The Thirteenth Century Lustred Vases*. Privately published, 1891.

Watson, Oliver. *Ceramics from Islamic Lands*. London: Thames & Hudson, 2004.

——. *Persian Lustre Ware*. London: Faber & Faber, 1985.

——. "Persian Lustre-Painted Pottery: The Rayy and Kashan Styles." *Transactions of the Oriental Ceramic Society* 40 (1976): 1–19.

——. "Report on the Glazed Ceramics." *Ar-Raqqa 1: Die frühislamische Keramik von Tall Aswad*, Peter A. Miglus, ed., pp. 81–87. Mainz am Rhein: Philipp von Zabern, 1999.

Whitehouse, David. "Maritime Trade in the Gulf: The 11th and 12th Centuries." *World Archaeology* 14/3 (1983): 328–34.

Wilkinson, Charles K. *Nishapur: Pottery of the Early Islamic Period*. New York: Metropolitan Museum of Art, 1973.

Williamson, Andrew. "Regional Distribution of Mediaeval Persian Pottery in the Light of Recent Investigations." In *Syria and Iran: Three Studies in Medieval Ceramics*, edited by James Allen and Caroline Roberts, pp. 11–22. Oxford Studies in Islamic Art 4. Oxford: Oxford University Press, 1987.

CATALOGUE OF ARTIFACTS IN THE EXHIBITION

Registration Number   *Object Description*

Discovering Islamic Culture: An Archaeologist's Perspective

OIM A115005	Lamp, earthenware with turquoise glaze
OIM A115007	Base of vessel, fritware decorated with minai technique over opaque white glaze
OIM A115060	Rim and neck of jar-shaped lamp, cream earthenware
OIM A115063	Cross tile, fritware with blue glaze
OIM A115066	Lamp, fritware painted in black under green glaze
OIM A115069	Lamp, fritware with green glaze
OIM A115073	Sherd, fritware luster painted over opaque white glaze outside, blue glaze inside
OIM A115074	Lamp fragment, earthenware with turquoise glaze
OIM A115080	Central base of lamp, fritware with turquoise glaze
OIM A115082	Handle of lamp, earthenware with turquoise glaze
OIM A115208	Base of vessel, fritware decorated with *minai* technique over opaque white glaze
OIM A115222	Lamp, earthenware with turquoise glaze
RH 5612	Watercolor painting of vase, fritware decorated with luster
RH 6064	Watercolor painting of bowl, fritware decorated in *minai* technique over opaque white glaze
RE 3114	Watercolor painting of lamp with turquoise glaze
RE 2763	Watercolor painting of lamp with green glaze
RH 5039	Watercolor painting of lamp with turquoise glaze
RH 5884	Watercolor painting of two tiles, one decorated in luster, the other in blue glaze
OIM A35530	Tile, molded fritware with turquoise glaze

Everyday Beauty

OIM A115056	Rim sherd of a cooking pot or jar, earthenware with incised decoration
OIM A115057	Rim sherd of a cooking pot or jar, earthenware with incised decoration
OIM A115059	Rim and neck of jug, earthenware with applied decoration, inset with small glazed ceramic fragments
OIM A115061	Rim sherd of vessel, cream earthenware with molded decoration
OIM A115062	Rim sherd of bowl, steatite or a similar stone, with incised decoration
OIM A115088	Rim sherd, fritware decorated with luster, inscription on edge of rim
OIM A115118	Bowl fragment, earthenware with turquoise glaze
OIM A115122	Jug, red earthenware with applied decoration, inset with small glazed ceramic fragments
OIM A115123	Bowl, red earthenware with incised decoration along edge of rim
OIM A115165	Sherd, fritware with incised decoration under turquoise glaze
OIM A115167	Sherd, fritware with incised decoration under green glaze
OIM A115179	Base of a cup, fritware with turquoise glaze
RH 4745	Watercolor painting of a bowl with incised decoration under a green glaze
RCi 4021	Watercolor painting of a bowl with a turquoise glaze
RG 3320	Watercolor painting of a bowl, fritware with luster decoration
RH 4578	Watercolor painting of a cup, fritware with molded decoration under turquoise glaze
RH 4818	Watercolor painting of a jug with incised decoration under turquoise glaze

Function and Decoration

OIM A115051	Rim and shoulder of a sphero-conical vessel
OIM A115053	Rim and shoulder of a sphero-conical vessel
OIM A115054	Rim and shoulder of a sphero-conical vessel
OIM A115067	Spout of ewer in the shape of an animal head, fritware with turquoise glaze
OIM A115071	Spout of ewer in the shape of an animal head, fritware with turquoise glaze
OIM A115161	Base and legs of an animal figure, fritware with blue glaze
OIM A115162	Base and legs of an animal figure, fritware with blue glaze
OIM A115168	Bowl, earthenware with green glaze
OIM A115169	Bowl, earthenware with green glaze
OIM A115170	Bowl, earthenware with green glaze
RH 5590	Watercolor painting of a bowl, fritware painted in luster over opaque white glaze
RH 6105	Watercolor painting of an elephant ceramic figure, fritware with turquoise glaze
RH 5548	Watercolor painting of a bowl, fritware painted with blue lines in transparent glaze

Links to a Wider World

OIM A115002	Base of bowl, earthenware with incised decoration under polychrome glaze
OIM A115003	Rim of bowl, earthenware with polychrome glaze
OIM A115012	Chinese celadon sherd with incised decoration under light green glaze
OIM A115013	Chinese celadon sherd with incised decoration under light green glaze
OIM A115022	Rim sherd, earthenware with a white slip and incised decoration under transparent glaze, with green pigment along edge
OIM A115065	Fragment of plate, fritware with incised decoration and painted with blue lines in a transparent glaze
OIM A115085	Rim sherd, fritware with incised decoration under blue glaze
OIM A115093	Fragment of bowl, earthenware with a white slip, painted in blue and black under transparent glaze
OIM A115094	Fragment of bowl, earthenware with a white slip, painted in black and turquoise under transparent glaze
OIM A115095	Sherd, earthenware with white slip, painted in black under transparent turquoise glaze
OIM A115098	Rim of bowl, earthenware with slip-painted decoration
OIM A115103	Rim of vessel, earthenware with polychrome glaze
OIM A115104	Fragment of bowl, earthenware with splash decoration in brown glaze
OIM A115111	Sherd, cream earthenware with incised decoration
OIM A115128	Base of bowl, earthenware with incised decoration under polychrome glaze
OIM A115129	Rim sherd, earthenware with opaque white glaze and decoration in blue
OIM A115131	Base of vessel, earthenware with polychrome glaze
OIM A115144	Sherd, earthenware with opaque white glaze and decoration in turquoise and blue
OIM A115145	Rim sherd, earthenware with opaque white glaze and decoration in turquoise
OIM A115146	Sherd, earthenware with slip-painted decoration
OIM A115150	Sherd, cream earthenware with incised decoration
OIM A115154	Rim of bowl, fritware with transparent glaze
OIM A115156	Rim of bowl, fritware with transparent glaze
OIM A115157	Rim of bowl, fritware with incised decoration with blue lines in transparent glaze
OIM A115166	Rim sherd, fritware with molded decoration under turquoise glaze
OIM A115184	Sherd, earthenware with white slip, painted in black under transparent turquoise glaze
OIM A115188	Rim of vessel, porcelain with blue and white glaze
OIM A115189	Base of vessel, earthenware with white slip, painted in blue and green under transparent glaze
OIM A115191	Base of vessel, earthenware with white slip, painted in blue, black, and green under transparent glaze
OIM A115194	Base of vessel, earthenware with white slip, painted in black under a transparent turquoise glaze
OIM A115252	Sherd, earthenware with opaque white glaze and decoration in turquoise
OIM A115256	Rim sherd, fritware with incised decoration under turquoise glaze
OIM A115261	Sherd, earthenware with molded decoration and transparent glaze
OIM A115262	Sherd, earthenware with molded decoration and transparent glaze
OIM A115263	Base of vessel, earthenware with incised decoration and slip-painting under transparent glaze

RH 4796	Watercolor painting of an *albarello*, earthenware with slip-painting under polychrome glaze
RE 3135	Watercolor painting of a bowl, with green splash decoration over opaque white glaze
Unknown	Watercolor painting of a bowl, earthenware with decoration in slip painting
RH 5179	Watercolor painting of a bowl, earthenware with white slip and incised decoration under a transparent glaze, with green pigment around rim
Unknown	Watercolor painting of a bowl, underglaze painted

Religious Inspirations

OIM A115008	Sherd, fritware decorated in *minai* technique over opaque white glaze
OIM A115010	Rim sherd, fritware decorated in *minai* technique over opaque white glaze
OIM A115018	Sherd, fritware decorated with luster over opaque white glaze
OIM A115019	Rim sherd, fritware painted in luster over opaque white glaze
OIM A115025	Sherd, fritware decorated in *minai* technique over opaque white glaze
OIM A115026	Rim sherd, fritware decorated in *minai* technique over opaque white glaze
OIM A115027	Rim sherd, fritware decorated in *minai* technique over opaque white glaze
OIM A115030	Rim sherd, fritware decorated in *minai* technique over opaque white glaze
OIM A115031	Sherd, fritware decorated in *minai* technique over opaque white glaze
OIM A115032	Sherd, fritware decorated in *minai* technique over opaque white glaze
OIM A115033	Sherd, fritware decorated in *minai* technique over opaque white glaze
OIM A115034	Rim sherd, fritware decorated in *minai* technique over opaque white glaze
OIM A115039	Sherd, cream earthenware with molded decoration
OIM A115040	Sherd, cream earthenware with incised decoration
OIM A115041	Sherd, cream earthenware with incised decoration
OIM A115042	Sherd, cream earthenware with incised and stamped decoration
OIM A115043	Sherd, cream earthenware with stamped decoration
OIM A115044	Sherd, cream earthenware with molded or incised decoration
OIM A115045	Sherd, cream earthenware with molded decoration
OIM A115047	Sherd, cream earthenware with molded decoration
OIM A115049	Sherd, cream earthenware with molded decoration
OIM A115125	Fragment of earthenware ceramic mold
OIM A115135	Sherd, fritware painted in luster over an opaque white glaze outside and blue glaze inside
OIM A115138	Sherd, earthenware with polychrome glaze, inscription
OIM A115147	Sherd, cream earthenware with molded decoration
OIM A115148	Sherd, cream earthenware with molded decoration
OIM A115149	Sherd, cream earthenware with molded decoration
OIM A115171	Jug, cream earthenware with incised decoration
OIM A115172	Jug, cream earthenware with incised decoration
OIM A115220	Sherd, fritware painted in black under transparent turquoise glaze
RH 6074	Watercolor of a bowl, fritware decorated in *minai* technique over opaque white glaze
RE 2828	Watercolor of a bowl, fritware painted in black under a transparent turquoise glaze
1975/510	Manuscript painting: Shirin meeting with Khusrau, 1525/1550, Iran. Opaque watercolor and gold on paper, 6 x 4 ¼ in. Collection of the Art Institute of Chicago, Gift of Ann McNear

Industry and Innovation

OIM A115011	Base of vessel, fritware painted painted with blue in an opaque white glaze, with luster over the glaze
OIM A115014	Rim of vessel, fritware painted in luster over an opaque white glaze
OIM A115023	Sherd, fritware painted with luster over an opaque white glaze
OIM A115079	Base of cup, fritware with a black slip and carved decoration under a transparent turquoise glaze
OIM A115084	Base of vessel, fritware painted in blue under a transparent glaze
OIM A115130	Base of bowl, fritware painted in luster over an opaque white glaze outside and blue inside
OIM A115132	Rim of vessel, fritware painted in luster over an opaque white glaze
OIM A115139	Sherd, earthenware painted in luster over an opaque white glaze

OIM A115140	Rim sherd, earthenware painted in luster over opaque white glaze
OIM A115141	Sherd, earthenware painted in luster over opaque white glaze
OIM A115142	Rim sherd, earthenware painted in luster over opaque white glaze
OIM A115143	Base of vessel, fritware painted in blue and black under transparent glaze
OIM A115185	Sherd, fritware with a black slip and carved decoration under transparent turquoise glaze
OIM A115186	Base of bowl, fritware with black slip and carved decoration under transparent turquoise glaze
OIM A115192	Sherd, fritware painted with luster over opaque white glaze
OIM A115193	Sherd, fritware with applied decoration and turquoise glaze
OIM A115199	Rim of vessel, fritware painted with blue in opaque white glaze, with luster over the glaze
OIM A115250	Sherd, earthenware with cream slip under green glaze
OIM A115251	Sherd, fritware with molded and incised decoration under blue glaze
OIM A115253	Base of vessel, fritware with purple glaze
OIM A115255	Sherd, molded fritware with turquoise glaze
OIM A115257	Sherd, fritware painted in luster over opaque white glaze
OIM A115260	Sherd, fritware painted in luster over opaque white glaze
OIM A115264	Rim sherd, fritware painted in luster over opaque white glaze
OIM A115265	Sherd, fritware painted in luster over opaque white glaze
OIM A115266	Sherd, fritware painted in luster over opaque white glaze
RB 979	Watercolor painting of a bowl, fritware with underglaze painting
RE 2835	Watercolor painting of a bowl, fritware painted in black under turquoise glaze
RH 4759	Watercolor painting of a jug, fritware painted in luster over opaque white glaze
RH 6433	Watercolor painting of a jug, fritware painted in luster over turquoise glaze
RH 6118	Watercolor painting of a bowl, fritware painted in luster over opaque white glaze
1980/334	Manuscript painting: A man's death outside a pottery shop. 1570/1580, Iran, Shiraz. Opaque watercolor on paper, 7 5/8 x 4 in. Collection of the Art Institute of Chicago, Gift of Ann McNear

Timeline

OIM A115028	Sherd, fritware with *minai* decoration over opaque white glaze
OIM A115048	Sherd, cream earthenware with molded decoration
OIM A115099	Rim sherd, earthenware with slip-painted decoration
OIM A115124	Rim of vessel, fritware with molded decoration under turquoise glaze
OIM A115136	Rim of a bowl, earthenware with white slip, painted in blue and black under transparent glaze
OIM A115180	Sherd, earthenware with incised decoration under green glaze
OIM A115221	Fragment of vessel, earthenware with molded decoration under green glaze